Your Outdoor Room

HOW TO DESIGN A GARDEN YOU CAN LIVE IN

Manoj Malde

FRANCES LINCOLN

Introduction

Outdoor spaces are sometimes undervalued and underutilized, but they undoubtedly play a very important role in our lives. Nature has a relaxing, calming influence on the senses and walking into a well-planned garden can take us away from the stresses of everyday life. For that short time, we enter another zone. Being in nature and part of nature is good for both our mental and physical wellbeing, and by valuing our health we also impart a value on this outdoor space. It certainly deserves the same level of respect and consideration as any other area of our home.

A garden must not sit in isolation, separated from the home. By extending the styling or colours of your interiors into your outdoor space you begin to develop a strong bond between the two, creating a harmonious link between inside and out. All homes and gardens should have this synergy, but it is even more important when you have a small garden or a balcony where, in effect, you remove that invisible boundary, uniting the whole space to make it feel bigger.

Most of us have a pretty good idea of how we want to decorate our home, but may break into a cold sweat when it comes to our garden. Not surprising, perhaps, when there is constant change going on outside. As the seasons turn, trees awaken, their foliage unfurls and then falls in autumn, while herbaceous plants grow and die back. It's no wonder people get confused when there are so many variables to consider and, to top it all, the ever-changing weather. Designing a garden can be overwhelming when you are starting from scratch. However, this book will not only help you to overcome your fears but offer guidance and give you the skills to turn your garden into a beautiful, healthy, thriving, outdoor living space that will bring you joy for years to come.

As a former fashion designer, I am used to working with colour, shape, form, texture and proportions – all wonderful skills I could transfer when I changed my career to garden design. However, at first, even I used to make many common mistakes when creating gardens. Whether you are a complete novice, have a newfound love of gardening, have bought your first property, or are a garden enthusiast but have never designed a garden, this book offers you an award-winning garden designer by your side to mentor you as you embark on this exciting journey.

How to use this book

As a garden designer I am often asked by friends, family and social media followers what they can do with their gardens. They may need help with a small area, a balcony, or they may have bought a new-build property and have a blank canvas to work with. These all offer great opportunities.

In this book I break down the process of designing a garden into simple step-by-step sections, which I hope you will find useful in creating your own beautiful outdoor space.

With my expert knowledge and insight, I will guide you through the whole design process, providing creative inspiration while helping you to push your own ideas further. I cover surveying the site, creating mood boards and colour palettes, choosing materials and plants, and, finally, the installation and maintenance of your garden. There are also tips on how to save money, while the easy-to-use format allows you to dip in and out of sections, depending on which stage you are at. I truly hope this book will help make your garden design journey a beautiful and enjoyable one.

First and foremost, always think of your garden as part of your home. A garden can be a place of seclusion, but often it is a social space where you can bring family and friends together.

Depending on the size, you may wish to divide it into areas for different purposes, and structure the design around who will be using it. For example, in the case of very young children, while the garden should be fun, safety will be important.

If elderly parents are part of the family unit, consider their safe movement through the space, especially where level changes are needed.

What do you *need* from your *garden*?

When redesigning an interior room, the first step is to think about the space, and garden designers use the same approach outside. One of the first questions I ask my clients is how they want to use their garden. Most people like to sit and relax in their outdoor space, but they may not have really thought much beyond that.

I have a questionnaire for clients that helps them to explore both the practical and creative points they need to consider. It's also important that they think about what they need to include in the garden. So, make a wish list of your desires but be realistic: a common mistake is to try to fit everything you want into the garden, which may then end up looking messy, cluttered and not the relaxing, calm space you hoped for. Spend some time thinking with pen and paper at hand, really getting to grips with the space. Here are some starter questions about your garden and how it could be used:

— Is entertaining in the garden a consideration?
— Do you enjoy cooking and eating outside?
— Would you prefer to sit in the shade?
— Are you a sun worshipper?
— Do you work from home and would you like to do this in the garden?
— How much time do you want to spend gardening?

- Are you keen to try growing some fruit and vegetables?
- Would you like wildlife to visit your garden?
- Is the garden overlooked and do you need privacy?
- Are there views that you would like to enhance or ugly buildings that you would prefer to hide?
- Are children going to use the garden?
- Will there be older visitors who will use the space?
- Do you have pets which will also use the garden?
- Which hardscape materials do you like?
- Is sustainability important for you?
- Do you have preferred colours?
- What time(s) of day are you likely to use the garden most?

There are also the practical, though essential, questions:

- Where will the bins be stored?
- Will you need a clothesline to hang your washing out?
- Is there side access from the front of the house to the back garden?
- If there is no side access, are there any other routes into the garden?
- Do you have bicycles and where will they be stored?
- Are there any planning regulations or Tree Preservation Orders (TPO) on existing trees that need to be considered?
- Which boundary hedge or fence are you responsible for?

How will you use your garden?

Make your wish list of wants and needs. These may include the following elements.

ENTERTAINMENT SPACES
Your garden can make a great entertainment space when the weather is good or, by adding a covered structure, you can prolong the time you spend outside throughout the year. Also consider what entertainment means to you. Is it sitting around a table eating, drinking and being merry with friends and family? Do you want to play games, listen to music and dance, watch a movie, or simply sit with your loved ones sipping a cold glass of rosé?

CHILDREN'S PLAY AREA
If you have children, do they require a space to play in the garden. This will depend on their age. If they are very young, then an area where they can use their imagination can be far more fun than bought play equipment. If they are older, they may prefer to go to the park to kick a ball around, in which case, you are free to do something else with the garden.

OUTDOOR GYM
If you are into fitness, you might go to the gym but also wish to do some exercises at home. You may want a proper gym studio, but consider the cost since they are not cheap. On the other hand, you

could simply include an area for a gym mat for yoga, Pilates, or calisthenics.

THE CHILLOUT ZONE

You could include a relaxing area for loungers or a sofa and, perhaps, a firepit to lend a cosy feel. If you have a small garden, you could use the same area for yoga or Pilates. How about using your chillout zone as an outdoor cinema? You will need a screen, but this can be as simple as a blank white wall, or you can install a pull-up screen and projector. A chillout zone works well under a pergola. Simply having a roof above you and the vertical posts of the structure mimics sitting in a room. It also helps to create a dedicated space for relaxing. There are some very good pergolas that can be bought off-the-shelf, from the powder-coated aluminium kind with louvers at the top that you can open and close, which can extend your use of the garden when it is drizzling outside, to timber structures that come as a kit.

COOKING & DINING

Ideally, you want to cook where you are going to eat. If space permits, you might consider an outdoor kitchen or, in a smaller garden, a compact mobile barbeque may be a better option. However, if your outdoor dining area is close to the kitchen, then you may not require an outdoor kitchen at all.

GARDEN BAR

With more people entertaining at home, garden bars have become very popular. They can be an extension of an outdoor kitchen, or you could turn an outdoor studio into a dedicated bar, rather like a pub at the bottom of your garden. You could even

SHEDS & OUTBUILDINGS

Storage for any gardener is a must. You will need a space to keep your tools and bags of compost. Sheds can look a little drab so you can either hide one behind a screen, paint it a beautiful colour, or make it into a feature with some plants in the front to blend it into the garden.

HOT TUB OR SAUNA

Hot tubs offer a great way to bring a small group of friends together to relax and socialize. They come in different styles and sizes, and range from inflatable types that you can store inside in winter to beautiful wood-clad, stove-heated pools. If budget and space allow, you could even consider an outdoor sauna cabin or barrel – add a deck around it and you also have a great place to throw down your yoga mat and do a downward dog.

include a juke box for entertainment. Where space is more limited, consider a flip-down table attached to a wall, some fold-up stools and a few wall shelves for glasses and drinks.

THE KITCHEN GARDEN

If you would like to grow your own fruit and vegetables, you may want to design a separate productive plot in the garden, if space allows. However, for those with a small garden or balcony, why not grow your edibles alongside your ornamental plants? And remember that some plants such as chillies and aubergines provide colour and beautiful shapes as well as food. Also use the vertical spaces in your garden and include a living wall of herbs and small annual crops, or grow an espaliered fruit tree against a wall or fence.

MAINTENANCE

Just as our homes need to be cleaned and tidied, so do our gardens. Consider how much time you have for maintenance and if a problem then design a garden that does not need much aftercare. The more manicured a garden is, the more maintenance it will require. A clover lawn or meadow will be less time-consuming than a perfect, striped lawn. Choose materials that do not need constant cleaning such as porcelain or limestone that has been pre-sealed. Create a planting scheme with easy-care evergreen shrubs such as *Pittosporum*, *Euonymus* and the dwarf mountain pine (*Pinus mugo*), together with long-flowering perennials such as *Salvia* 'Royal Bumble' or *Coreopsis verticillata* 'Moonbeam' and ornamental grasses, including *Panicum*, *Pennisetum* and *Calamagrostis*.

GARDEN ESSENTIALS

Elements that you consider essential for your garden will partly depend on the size of the space, but the following will provide a strong foundation for your design:

— **Healthy soil** This will give your plants the best chance to establish and thrive (see p.43).

— **Good drainage** The biggest killer of plants is cold wet soil, unless they are bog plants or aquatics of course.

— **Plants** Aim for 60 per cent of your garden to be planted. A garden is not a garden without plants, and I always recommend a tree where space allows.

— **A journey and a destination** A journey can be created by a single level change or, in the case of a balcony, maybe something that you must walk around.

— **Seating** After all, a garden should be a place where you can relax and have some me time'.

— **Storage** You will need a place to put your tools, gardening gloves and a bag of compost.

What is your budget?

It is important to have an approximate budget in mind so that you do not set your heart on a spectacular garden that will end up blowing the bank. This will help you to make decisions about the materials, plants and structures you can afford, but remember that sometimes a limited budget can also bring innovation and creativity to the design, while ensuring you focus on what is really essential.

Keep in mind that a new garden does not have to be built and planted in one go. Knowing your budget can help you plan in phases. First, put the bones of your garden into place: the hard landscaped areas, any bases for structures, the electrical cables and structural planting such as trees and shrubs. Your second phase can include the installation of structures such as sheds, a garden studio, arches, pergolas, arbours and water features, and the last phase can be the soft scaping – the planting areas for climbers, ferns, grasses and perennials. A good tip is to buy small plants and install them at the right time and they will quickly fill out. Doing as many jobs yourself will also help to stretch your budget further, and working in phases can help you to fit it into your schedule.

What is the theme of your garden?

Our homes reflect our personality and, likewise, we should also put our own stamp on our gardens. Thinking in terms of a theme will help you to select colours, materials and furnishings. It also allows your personality to come through, just as it would when decorating a room in your home. You may have a favourite artist whose work you love. You might have had a wonderful holiday abroad and want a garden to remind you of your time there, or you may love a particular culture and its traditions. The list of themes is endless but here are some examples to get you thinking. However, do not limit yourself to these ideas; let your creative juices flow and feel free to choose your own theme.

- **Bohemian rhapsody:** full of colour taking inspiration from the hippy vibes of the 1970s.
- **The tropical jungle:** lush leafy foliage that reminds you of exotic holidays.
- **An English cottage:** rural references fused with pretty pastel florals.
- **The Impressionists:** moody tones of an impressionist painting.
- **An African safari:** hot desert colours, animal prints and the richness of African culture.
- **Enchanted Marrakech:** colours and patterns of the medina.
- **Shabby chic vintage:** elements and styling that reference yesteryear.

Where can I source inspiration for my theme?

There are many different places you can source inspiration for themes. Set your sights beyond gardens: go to galleries and exhibitions, rummage through magazines and books, think about holidays and public spaces you've visited. The inspiration for my garden 'Beneath a Mexican Sky' at the Chelsea Flower Show in 2017 (see bottom right) came from looking at the work of Mexican architect Luis Barragán. I also find holidays are a great source of ideas. If you have been to Kenya on a safari holiday, you will have experienced not just the savannah but the wildlife and the flora and fauna in the gardens at the safari resorts. You will also have seen some of the colourful Kenyan tribes such as Maasai, Samburu or Turkana (see top right), all of which can be used as inspiration for your outdoor space.

Of course, gardens themselves can provide great ideas, particularly if you want a specific style. For example, if you are designing a Japanese-style garden, there are some wonderful books on the subject and beautiful Japanese gardens to visit, such as those at Tatton Park near Manchester (see left), Capel Manor in north London and further abroad the Japanese Tea Garden in San Francisco and Mejiro Garden in Tokyo, all packed with great ideas.

If your intention is to connect your indoor and outdoor spaces, source inspiration for the garden by looking at your own home decor.

Should I create a mood board?

Making a mood board helps to build and strengthen the look, feel and ambience you want to create in your garden. A mood board is a series of images and materials arranged to evoke a particular look, style, or concept of the finished garden. As a garden designer, it is my reference point from which I can take specific ideas. It helps me to select colour palettes which I can then use for the planting scheme, furniture, soft furnishings and paints.

Mood board

When I created 'Beneath a Mexican Sky', the starting point was the bold colours of Barragán's architecture (see top left, opposite). My design told the story of his struggle to be recognized by the architectural world, and I used his famous tangerine and rouge-pink walls as a backdrop to the garden, balanced with a neutral café au lait coloured wall. Shades, tints and tones of these colours were also introduced into the planting scheme, which included drought-tolerant species that are used to growing in heat and dry, impoverished soil. I brought Barragán's love of horses into the garden with a sculpture of a horse's head in copper wire and a water feature that was inspired by one of his equine pools. Even the soft furnishings tied in with the garden's colour scheme.

How do I create a mood board?

When creating a mood board, first give it a theme title and either make one or a few, dividing them into sub-sections such as planting and hard landscaping. You can now use your mood board/s as your reference to help you stay true to the theme in all aspects of your design. At the start of my design career, mood boards could only be made by physically pinning images to a foam board. These could be edited until you were sure that the boards represented the intended theme, mood, details and colour. You can still make a board like this and collate objects and images to swap in or out, or you can create a digital version using specialist design software. Photoshop is also useful for creating mood boards.

When creating your mood board, look for images that you really love and fit your theme. These can be photographs, yours or from magazines, or pictures you have found on the internet that represent the colours, details and moods you wish to convey in your design. It helps to start with an excess of images, then edit them down, and you can also change them as the design develops.

Other items to hone your colour theme include chips of coloured paper – sample paint cards are ideal for this – fabric swatches or embroidery yarns.

With your mood board in place, you can now start work on the physical creation of your garden.

Colour *palettes*

When I ask my clients what they would like in the garden, top of the list is colour. However, what they are really referring to is the flora but colours do not just have to be about flowers. You can inject colour into your garden in many ways. Take, for instance, Le Jardin Majorelle in Marrakech in Morocco, a bold garden created by the French artist Jacques Majorelle, and later bought by the fashion designer Yves Saint-Laurent and his partner Pierre Bergé. The vibrant ultramarine walls of the building and sunflower yellow jali window grills make a real impact on the space, and could offer inspiration for furniture in fun colours rather than the usual timber or rattan. If that is a step too far, then think about accessorizing the furniture with cushions in bright colours or vibrant prints. Colourful glazed pots or powder-coated metal containers can also inject colour into an outdoor space.

There is a lot of snobbery about colour, but our world is filled with it, so why not embrace it and have fun with it in your garden?

What is colour?

Cézanne said, 'Colour is where our brain and the universe meet.' When we talk about colour what we are really referring to is the effect of light on an object, which can change with the seasons and time of day. This is why we all experience colour in different ways.

Colour is a powerful tool used by designers to express ideas and emotions and to create a feeling within a space. It can affect moods, bring back memories and cause reactions. It is also tied to our emotions and from the time we are born we are introduced to the language of colour. For example, 'tickled pink', 'feeling blue', 'green with envy', all reflect our views of the world through colour. However, the way we perceive colours and what we associate with them can vary, depending on our traditions and cultural background – a deep orange always reminds me of an African sunset, for example, but I associate combinations of pink and orange with India.

Colours can also influence the mood of your garden. Hot colours such as red, yellow and orange that demand attention are deemed to be energetic colours. Blues, greens and lilacs have a calming influence. Jewel colours, including purples, magenta and burgundy, are considered rich, aristocratic and opulent. Designers also employ colour to create a connection between the garden and the people using it.

In a garden, colour can be introduced through painted walls, fences, structures, pots, soft furnishing, furniture, as well as flowers.

The colour basics

To understand colour, we need to go back to basics. You may remember learning about the colour wheel back in school. Red, yellow and blue are the primary colours which cannot be created by mixing other colours. Secondary colours are formed by combining two of the primary colours: red and yellow creates orange; yellow and blue gives you green; blue mixed with red makes purple. Tertiary colours are created by mixing primary and secondary colours. Adding grey to a base colour will give you tones of that colour, while shades are created by adding black. Tints are the result of adding white to the base colour. When referring to hue, one is referring to the dominant primary colour that the actual colour leans towards.

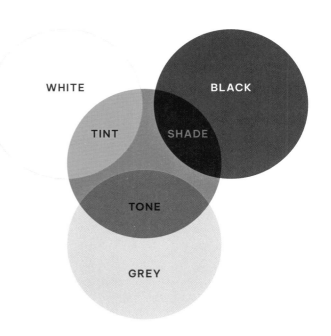

What is colour harmony?

Designers will often talk about harmonious colours. Harmony is created when we put together closely related groups of colours that have the same or a similar tint, shade, hue, or tonal value. However, place these too close together and the colours could merge to make quite a dull space. It is better to vary the values in tone, shade, tint, or hue to create a sharper, crisper image. This way the colours also support each other. For example, reds, oranges and yellows create a show-stopping hot colour palette, but while they work in harmony together, they are not restful as a palette of colours. They sing at the top of their voices. They exude heat and energy. Think dahlias, rudbeckias, heleniums, crocosmia and cannas in the borders. If you want a more restful palette, a combination of cool blues, violets, mauves, lilacs and a sprinkling of white will give a more calming harmony of colours. Demure and shy, these colours will create a contemplative space. Although there is rarely a true blue colour in nature you can use *Salvia patens*, *Geranium wallichianum* 'Havana Blues', agapanthus, cornflowers, asters, *Caryopteris* and *Plumbago*.

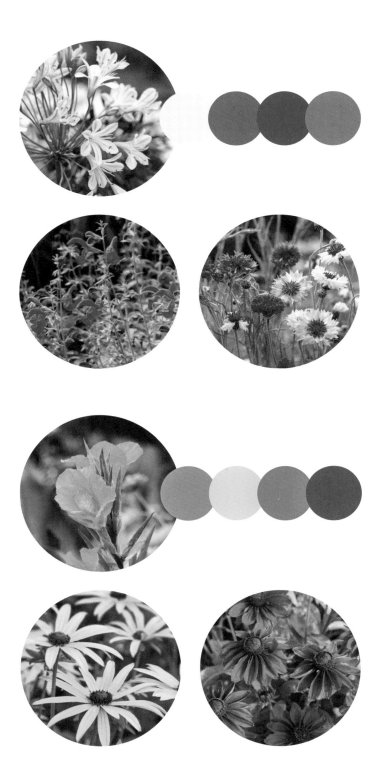

Choosing complementary colours

Like me, you may prefer to use colours that complement each other rather than harmonize. Complementary colours are those that sit opposite each other on the colour wheel. For example red and green sit opposite each other creating a high colour contrast.

To explain this further, let's go back to some of the themes I have suggested previously. For example, 'An African Safari' immediately reminds me of my holiday travelling across the dusty plains of the Maasai Mara. The red iron-rich earth and the flaxen colours of the dry grass; the rich colours of the Maasai's beaded adornments crafted in crimson, canary and tangerine, with touches of emerald and lapis; and the rich, fiery colours of the African sunset all provide inspiration.

These colours can so easily be translated into a stunning outdoor space. Use complementary, contrasting colours for hard landscaping such as bricks, clay pavers, the sandy tones of gravel and rusty tones of weathered steel. I would also add some animal prints using soft furnishings and outdoor rugs. And how about recycling some oil drums to use as plant containers and painting them in zebra, giraffe, or leopard skin patterns? For your planting borders, think of hot colours like red, crimson oxblood, vermillion, russet, tangerine, fuchsia pink and zesty yellows sitting with the cooler greens and emeralds of the foliage. Balance the heat of these colours with some softer colours like vanilla cream and mango sorbet.

Whichever colour scheme you choose, it can be extended into the colours of the furniture and soft furnishings.

How do I create a colour palette?

Firstly, do not be afraid of colour. Have fun with it. There is too much snobbery around colour – what is right, what is wrong, what is tasteful and what is not. Do not forget that this is your private, personal space and the colours you choose must bring you joy.

To create your colour palette, play about with different hues on your mood board. I often lay out my colours and then revisit them the next day. Looking at them with a fresh pair of eyes helps me to assess whether they are working as a group or if some of them need changing.

You can also use a few tester paint pots to make swatches and leave them in different areas of the garden to see how the natural light affects the different colours throughout the day. For 'Beneath a Mexican Sky' I tried three different shades for each colour, living with them for four months. The orange colour I

thought I might use started to look dirty in the spring sunshine , but the shade of orange I thought would not work lifted as the days got brighter.

When designing the 'RHS & Eastern Eye Garden of Unity' for the Chelsea Flower Show 2023, I wanted to bring some of my garden design style into the community space that this garden represents. I pinned on my mood board an image of vertical perspex bands in pinks and oranges with just a few clear and aubergine bands dotted through them, and these were the colours that inspired the garden's bold backdrop. As a community garden I wanted the space to lift people's spirits. I took the tangerine and rouge-pink colours from the image and had paints mixed in a slightly softer hue. These were balanced with ivory and aubergine, which I used in other elements of the garden to ground and support the stronger colours.

2

Planning your new garden

Planning a garden is about unlocking the space and making it work for you, so it pays to spend time assessing it before you begin. Plan your garden on paper rather than going straight into the garden, and avoid the common mistake of working on each area in isolation. Working on the design of the whole garden will create flow, harmony and cohesion, and prevent costly mistakes.

Every element will be designed to be in the right place, making the garden feel comfortable and inviting. So where do you start?

Preparation for the *design*

Planning is key and by mapping out each stage, you reduce the risk of deviating from your original vision. The number of plans suggested here may seem excessive but, trust me, each of these layers plays a crucial role in the final design.

Understanding the preparations needed before the design process is invaluable. There are a few plans you'll need to develop, but by the end of this chapter, you will be a dab hand at producing the following list:

1 **Site survey** The plan of your existing garden with all the measurements drawn to scale.

2 **Site analysis** After surveying the site, you mark your findings on this plan. Your assessments could include damp or dry areas, shadows from trees and buildings, the north point, drainage issues, and any other details that could impact the site and your new design.

3 **Concept plan** Showing the intended elements of the new design, this plan includes the shape and position of the patio and planting borders, location of other seating areas, position of the shed, where new trees might be located, and any other elements that you intend to introduce into your new garden.

4 **Master plan** This plan shows all the details of your garden design to scale. It includes paving slabs, pathways, seating areas with furniture, sheds, barbeques and structural planting such as trees and shrubs. Your boundary line will be drawn to scale, too, be it a fence, wall or hedge. And everything will be labelled correctly with information about the materials to be used and their dimensions.

5 **Level plan** You will also need a plan that shows the existing and new levels.

6 **Setting out plan** This plan has all the measurements marked on it, from which you will work when marking out the garden on the ground.

7 **Planting plan** The plan will have every single plant marked as a circle in its correct position. These will be drawn to scale to represent the eventual spread of the plant.

8 **Lighting plan** Different colour dots will represent the different types of light fittings. The dots will be positioned in the correct locations, while circuit lines will indicate which lights will be joined to what circuit.

Marking existing and new levels
I tend to make a copy of the master plan without the labelling. I then mark on the copy the existing levels in blue with a blue dot beside each level. The new levels are marked in red with a small red triangle beside each new level. Not only does this save any confusion but should you need to give a black and white copy of the plan to anyone, the symbols make everything clear – so do clarify on the plan that a dot is an existing level and a triangle is a new level.

Creating a site survey

This survey brings together all the relevant information about the site that you will need to create your design, such as the location of steps, walls, drainage covers, drainpipes and thresholds. It should also include the level changes, aspect (which direction the garden faces), soil type, and even the surroundings beyond your boundaries. Your site plan does not have to be too neat – that will come later – but the information must be legible and clear to avoid confusion.

STEP 1 – MEASURING FOR A SITE SURVEY

Sketch the shape of your garden on a piece of paper and then look at what you have. Measure the boundaries of your garden (including height of boundary walls, fences or hedges) and mark these on the sketch. You may need a second pair of hands to help you with measuring. That friend will also come in handy when you need to know the approximate height of a tree. Ask your helper to stand next to the tree and take a photo. Then measure the height of your friend and calculate how many times he or she fits along the height of the tree in your picture. Once you know the height of your friend you can also fairly accurately calculate how many times they would fit across the spread of the canopy.

Measure and draw in all the existing features of your garden such as patio, terraces, steps, downpipes, taps, electric points, the position of trees and shrubs, shed and other structures, water features and manhole covers. Also note the depth

SITE SURVEY

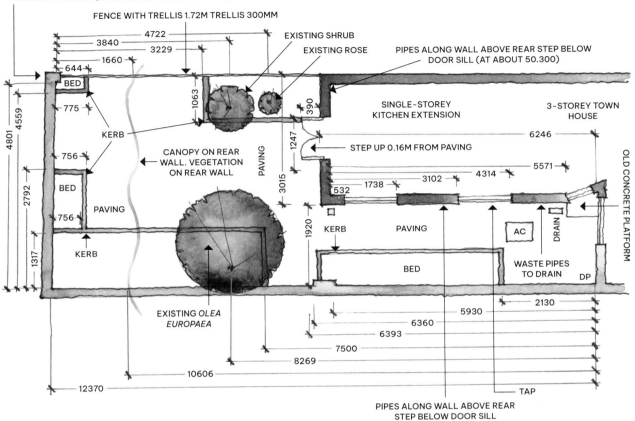

WALL WITH TRELLIS (WALL 2.27M / TRELLIS 800MM)

FENCE WITH TRELLIS 1.72M TRELLIS 300MM

EXISTING SHRUB

EXISTING ROSE

PIPES ALONG WALL ABOVE REAR STEP BELOW
DOOR SILL (AT ABOUT 50.300)

4722
3840
3229
1660
644

BED

775

4801 4559

KERB

756

2792

BED

756

PAVING

1317

KERB

1063

CANOPY ON REAR
WALL. VEGETATION
ON REAR WALL

PAVING

1247

390

3015

1920

SINGLE-STOREY
KITCHEN EXTENSION

3-STOREY TOWN
HOUSE

STEP UP 0.16M FROM PAVING

6246

5571

4314

3102

1738

532

KERB

PAVING

BED

AC

DRAIN

WASTE PIPES
TO DRAIN

DP

OLD CONCRETE PLATFORM

EXISTING *OLEA
EUROPAEA*

2130

5930

6360

6393

7500

8269

10606

12370

TAP

PIPES ALONG WALL ABOVE REAR
STEP BELOW DOOR SILL

Materials needed for a site survey

- A3 paper
- HB Pencil
- Ruler
- Eraser
- Some fine liner felt pens. I use 0.3mm
- Hard metal tape measure, preferably 8m/26ft long
- Soft wax-coated tape measure that reals out
- Compass. There are many free apps that you can download on your mobile phone
- Spade to dig test holes
- Watering can
- Soil test kit
- Stakes
- String
- Spirit level
- Camera
- And a friend or assistant to hold the other end of the tape measure

of the manholes. Include the walls of your house, doors and windows at ground floor level that face the garden (after all, views into the garden are important), and draw the doors to indicate in which direction they open. Note on your sketch the height of the threshold, windowsills and the DPC (damp proof course).

From inside the house, look out at the garden through doors and windows (including upstairs) observing where the best views are. It is worth taking photos, too, as reminders when you commence designing.

STEP 2 – TRIANGULATIONS

Gardens are rarely a perfect square or rectangle. One of my first jobs was to design a front garden. I thought the garden gate was aligned with the front door, but when I drew the survey, I was very surprised to find that this was not the case. Even my client was surprised – she had lived there for many years without noticing.

Without making things overly complicated, triangulations will help you plot the points of those odd shapes. For instance, the right side of your garden may be slightly longer than the left and protrude out by 30 degrees. Taking measurements from both corners of the house to the right-hand corner will help you plot that measurement when it comes to drawing your survey properly. I suggest that you do this with both left and right rear corners.

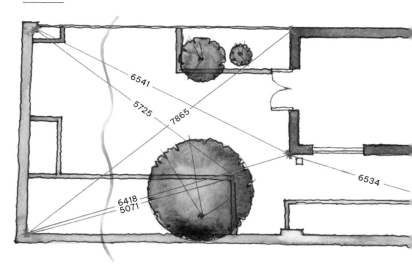

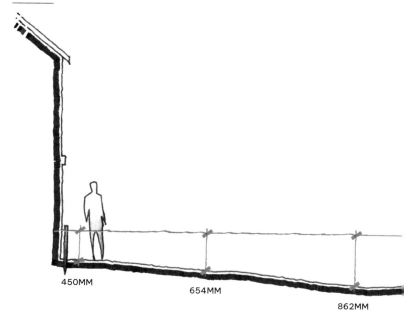

STEP 3 – LEVEL CHANGES AND SPOT LEVELS

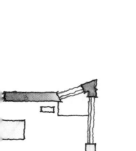

Most gardens will have a level change somewhere, even if it is stepping out over the threshold and down onto the patio. Some gardens may include a slope in one direction or another. Most professional garden designers will carry out a survey themselves to assess level changes or, if a plot is particularly steep or problematic, they may engage a topographical surveyor who will have more sophisticated equipment. However, in most cases, you can plot your garden's level changes yourself using some stakes, a string line, tape measure and a spirit level.

a. Put a stake in the ground near the house and then another at the other end of the garden.

b. Tie a string line from one stake to the other.

c. Place your spirit level on top of the string and make sure the bubble is in the centre. If it is, then your string is perfectly level.

d. If not, then you need to adjust the string, checking your spirit level until the line is perfectly straight.

e. Once it is level, use your tape measure to record the distance between the string line and the ground.

f. You could do this along the string line at 1m/ 39in intervals. These measurements are called spot levels.

g. It is worth doing this along several lengths and widths of the garden.

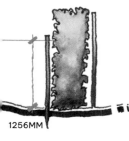

1256MM

Having this information may help you decide where best to create a designed level change in your garden. Any areas raised higher than 30cm/12in above ground level require planning permission.

STEP 4 – ASPECT OF THE GARDEN

The aspect of a garden is simply another way of describing the direction it faces. South-facing plots usually receive lots of sun and, conversely, north-facing gardens are generally shady and cooler. East- and west-facing areas get the best of both worlds, with some hours of sun each day and some hours of shade. Make a note of the areas of the garden that are in sun and shade at different times of the day, which will help you to decide where to create special seating areas, although that shouldn't be a problem for 'sundowners' chasing the last light of the day if they have a west-facing garden. Your aspect will also determine which plants will thrive in your garden. For example, Mediterranean plants such as lavender that need a hot, sunny situation will not survive in the shade in a north-facing garden and may even struggle if your plot faces east. There are some great compass apps that can help you locate the north point, which you can mark on your sketch with an 'N' and an arrow.

STEP 5 – THE SOIL

Soil is a very complex subject, and understanding it is key to creating a beautiful garden. If your soil is a rich brown colour with small stones, then you probably have good topsoil. If the soil is sandy, pale or grey in colour, then your soil is poor quality and may need improving. However, this is not the end of the world as there are certain plants that will grow in impoverished soil. Sometimes it is more difficult to grow plants in sticky clay that is high in nutrients but holds water and is slow to warm up in the spring.

It is also important to test the acidity or alkalinity of your soil, known as its pH value. There are some inexpensive soil kits that you can easily use; simply follow the instructions on the packaging. This information will help you to determine what plants will grow successfully and those that may struggle. It is about right plant, right place. If your soil is not neutral, then it is worth noting down or, better still, taking photos of the plants that are already growing well in your garden and the neighbours'. You could always show the photos to a good nursery who will be happy to help identify the plants. Camellias, rhododendrons, azaleas and blue-flowering hydrangeas thrive in acidic soil. Lavender, wisteria, daphne and achillea prefer alkaline soil.

STEP 6 – THE SURROUNDINGS

Observe the surroundings and check if you have any beautiful views from your property to the landscape beyond your boundaries. If there are, you may want to incorporate these and make them part of your garden, a technique known as 'borrowed landscape'. On the other hand, the views might be ugly, in which case you may want to hide them and restrict your focus to your own space.

Also check if any neighbouring trees are impacting your garden. A deciduous tree canopy in full leaf will cast a shadow from late spring to autumn that may restrict the growth of many plants, while the dense shade and dry soil beneath conifers prevents most plants from growing near them.

If your garden is on a slope, mark the direction with an arrow pointing upwards on your site plan and write 'upward direction'. Rainwater may run off your neighbour's garden on one side and into yours, or along the length of your plot if it slopes in that direction, creating an area that is constantly damp, so mark that on the plan too.

ASSESSING SOIL

The best way to assess your soil is to get your hands dirty and have a good feel of it. Dig up a sample from just below the surface and rub it between your fingers. If it feels sticky and holds together when you squeeze it, you probably have clay. If the soil feels gritty, then you have sandy soil. Soils with a high percentage of sand have good drainage, while clay-rich soils tend to be poorly drained and may be prone to waterlogging. Squeeze the soil and then open your hand. Now prod the lump. If it stays in a solid lump, it has a high clay content and will be difficult to work, while young plants may struggle to establish in it. However, you can improve it by digging in some horticultural gravel, or, better still, spreading a thick layer (or mulch) of organic matter such as homemade compost or well-rotted manure over the surface each year. This will help to open up the soil and improve drainage. If the lump falls apart the moment you open your hand, it means your soil contains a high proportion of sand. The same treatment using layers of organic matter will also help these light soils to retain more water and nutrients. If areas of your garden look patchy or the growth of plants looks poor, there could be a more serious issue such as builder's rubble buried underground, a high water table or drainage issues caused by heavily compacted soil. It would be worth investigating.

Also do a percolation test in three or four different places in the garden to assess the drainage capacity of your soil. Dig test holes approximately 40cm/16in deep. Fill each hole with water and then observe how quickly they drain. If the water drains straightaway, you have free-draining soil. If the water just sits in the hole and does not drain away, there is a drainage problem, which may be due to the soil type, compaction, or a high water table.

So long as your garden is not a quagmire all year round, I would suggest improving the soil with organic matter as described above. The organic matter is carried down into the soil by worms where substances in it coat sand particles, helping them to retain water and nutrients. It also helps to stick tiny clay particles together, creating larger aggregates with more gaps between them, which allows oxygen to reach the roots and water to drain away more easily. Add mulches over several years for the best effects. However, if drainage is a major issue you may need to engage a professional landscaper to create a soakaway at the lowest level in your garden and lay land drains leading to it.

It is also worth smelling your soil: sweet and earthy are good signs; a sour, fermented smell is bad. Sour odours could also be down to poor drainage. When plants sit in waterlogged soil, their roots drown due to the lack of oxygen and then rot, while the smell is caused by anaerobic bacteria that break down the organic matter in these airless conditions. Follow the points above to improve the soil drainage.

How do I create a site survey to scale?

Having measured your garden and noted all the information you need, you can now create a neatly drawn site survey to scale.

I always explain to clients that garden designers create plans to scale in a similar way to architects, and this is exactly what you will be doing on a piece of A3 graph paper. Each square on the paper can represent a 1m/3ft unit measurement. Lay a piece of A3 tracing paper over the graph paper and secure it in place with masking tape. You are now ready to draw an accurate scaled survey using the measurements and information on your rough sketch.

Draw your site survey in pencil first and then ink it in later when you are completely satisfied that everything is correct. Using different line weights when inking in will help to clarify the hierarchy in your drawing. Stay with me and I shall explain: imagine what a bird looking down on your property would see. The house stands out because it is the tallest item: draw this with the 0.7 micro-graphic pen. Next are the trees, which are drawn with the 0.5 pen. Then use the 0.35 pen for the shrubs, the 0.25 pen for herbaceous perennials and the 0.13 pen can be used for anything at ground level such as patios. Using the next nib size down for each level will help create this hierarchy and make your drawing easier to read.

For triangulation measurements spread the compass from point to lead, using the same scaled measurement as the triangulation you want to mark in. Put the metal point of the compass at the corner

Materials for drawing your plans to scale
— A3 Graph paper
— A3 Tracing paper
— Ruler
— H and HB Pencils
— Eraser
— Compass with lead to draw triangulations
— Micro-graphic pens 0.13, 0.25, 0.35, 0.5 & 0.7
— Peelable masking tape
— A circle template (with various circle sizes)

of the house and gently mark an arc on the side where you want to plot your measurement. Repeat this with your other triangulation measurement for the same plot. Where the two arcs cross over, you have the point you want to plot.

Indicate the north point. You now have an exact scaled site survey plan (bird's eye) view of your existing garden. Before proceeding with the spot levels and measurements, I suggest taking several copies of this plan or even scan it and save it onto your computer. A copy can be used to create your site analysis plan later and saves you drawing everything again.

Now complete your site survey plan by adding all the measurements, spot levels and labels. You may want to create abbreviations for certain elements such as MH for manhole, DP for downpipe, RW for retaining wall, and so on. Make a key of these on the side of the drawing so you do not forget what they mean.

With the correct dimensions of patios, paths and other landscaping features, you can calculate the quantity of materials you will need. Some suppliers will also help you if you give them accurate measurements. If you guesstimate the quantities, you run the risk of over- or under-ordering. Either way, this is a waste of time and money. Refer to 'How do I stretch my budget?' on page 110.

Site Analysis

Once you have drawn the scaled site survey plan, use one of the copies you took earlier and transfer all the information about the surroundings onto it with an HB pencil. Mark in directions of good or bad views beyond the boundary, plus any shady areas, noting the cause of shade. Add the damp areas and any drainage issues, indicating the cause if you know what it is. Label any existing trees or shrubs you would like to keep and, if there is a wind tunnel from any direction, note this with a direction arrow.

The plan should also include information about the soil, including its pH, texture (sand or clay) and what it smells like. The more relevant information you have, the better. If your neighbour's garden is on higher or lower level, then note this too, plus the level difference, if you can.

Designing with patterns and shapes
Designers think of the garden space as having areas of mass and void. Mass means three-dimensional areas of bulk that you cannot walk into, such as planting borders, sheds or trees. The voids are the flatter areas that are often hardscaped. These are patios, terraces, decks and pathways, and they also include lawns and open water.

Before getting into the finer details, garden designers start with lines, squares, circles and other geometrics that create patterns and shapes. While you can use the existing shapes in your garden and just modify them, working with a blank canvas may help you to divide and make better use of the space. You can create symmetry and geometry using simple lines, squares and rectangles, which will evoke calm. Alternatively, circles and curves produce dynamic, energetic shapes that create a sense of drama.

Creating your concept plan

Lay a piece of A3 tracing paper over your site survey to scale. Using your HB pencil, mark out the house, windows, doors, boundaries and any elements that you have decided to keep. Once you have done this, put aside the site survey. Start developing your concept plan on the A3 tracing paper. Using your HB pencil draw shapes and patterns in the area that represents your garden space. Fill in certain shapes that you feel could work as mass and leave others unfilled. Remember this is the experimental stage of developing the design of your garden. It is worth trying several different versions of this. By laying one drawing over another, dynamic shapes can begin to emerge. Once you are happy with a particular drawing, you can develop this into your concept plan. I tend to do mine in pencil and keep them quite sketchy.

Lay the sketch that you are happy with, over a piece of A3 graph paper aligning the property to the grid. Use this as a guide to refine and develop your concept plan. The lines that you have drawn can be refined, extended and used to join one area to another. Take your time with this. As you do this you will see the shapes develop. You may choose to make certain shapes bigger, others smaller and have spaces in between. As your shapes develop you will be able to decide on areas that will work well as planting borders, patios, terraces, pathways, or water features. Once you're happy with the concept plan, move on to the master plan.

Creating your master plan

The master plan is an accurate representation of the whole garden but with more details than the concept plan. Drawn to scale, so that you can be sure that all the elements fit comfortably, it will be the plan you work from to create your new garden. It includes paving slabs, pathways, seating areas with furniture, shed, barbeque, and structural planting such as trees and shrubs. Even your boundary line, be it a fence or hedge, will be drawn to scale and labelled correctly (see Labelling the master plan, opposite). To start, lay a piece of A3 tracing paper on top of your concept plan. Do not remove the graph paper with the grid – you still need that.

Using your H pencil, include any existing elements of the garden that you plan to keep. After deciding which materials you plan to use for paving and paths and noting the dimensions of slabs, bricks, pavers, or timber you can start developing the new design that you drew on your concept plan by filling the shapes with the materials to scale. Your shapes may require slight adjustments in size to reduce cutting and wastage. Remember that when you are drawing stone slabs, bricks, or pavers, you will need to adjust the dimensions to include the pointing gaps. As these gaps are too small to draw, designers simply include them within the dimensions of the materials.

Refer to your site survey plan. Are there any slopes that require cutting into to create steps that will take you from one level to the next? Even on a shallow slope, consider a simple one-step level change, which will introduce more character and a journey through the garden. All steps should be marked with an arrow in the direction you would climb the steps up. The steps should also be numbered, starting with zero at the bottom step and finishing in numerical order at the very top step.

Also include all the new elements to scale that you plan to introduce, such as trees, a water feature, containers, raised borders, a shed, screens, or hedges. Once you are happy with all the details, you are ready to ink your drawing. Remember to use the different thicknesses of micro-graphic pens to create the same hierarchy on your master plan that you used for the site survey plan (see p.44). When you are finished, take a couple of copies of the master plan, which you can use to create your setting out plan and planting plan.

Labelling the master plan

Now you can start labelling your master plan. Label everything, including all the existing and new spot levels, as well as each element such as the patio, paths, shed, arbour and pergola.

To prevent the drawing looking cluttered, write the labels around and not on the plan. Draw a line pointing from text to the item on the plan. If still too cluttered, you can always take an extra copy without the labelling and use this to mark on the existing and new spot levels.

You can also include more detailed information in a panel to one side of the drawing. For example, for the patio, you could add the material, supplier, dimensions, measurement of pointing gaps between pavers, colour, code references, the pattern in which the slabs are to be laid and how the foundation is to be constructed. Designers include these details for all the new materials and elements of the garden.

THE MASTER PLAN

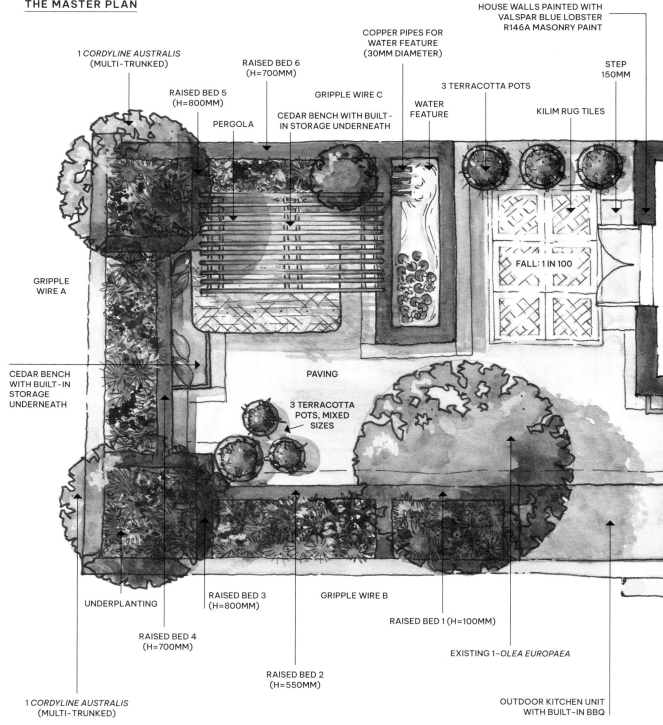

1 *CORDYLINE AUSTRALIS* (MULTI-TRUNKED)

RAISED BED 5 (H=800MM)

PERGOLA

RAISED BED 6 (H=700MM)

CEDAR BENCH WITH BUILT-IN STORAGE UNDERNEATH

GRIPPLE WIRE C

COPPER PIPES FOR WATER FEATURE (30MM DIAMETER)

WATER FEATURE

3 TERRACOTTA POTS

KILIM RUG TILES

HOUSE WALLS PAINTED WITH VALSPAR BLUE LOBSTER R146A MASONRY PAINT

STEP 150MM

GRIPPLE WIRE A

CEDAR BENCH WITH BUILT-IN STORAGE UNDERNEATH

PAVING

3 TERRACOTTA POTS, MIXED SIZES

FALL: 1 IN 100

UNDERPLANTING

RAISED BED 3 (H=800MM)

GRIPPLE WIRE B

RAISED BED 4 (H=700MM)

RAISED BED 1 (H=100MM)

EXISTING 1-*OLEA EUROPAEA*

RAISED BED 2 (H=550MM)

1 *CORDYLINE AUSTRALIS* (MULTI-TRUNKED)

OUTDOOR KITCHEN UNIT WITH BUILT-IN BBQ

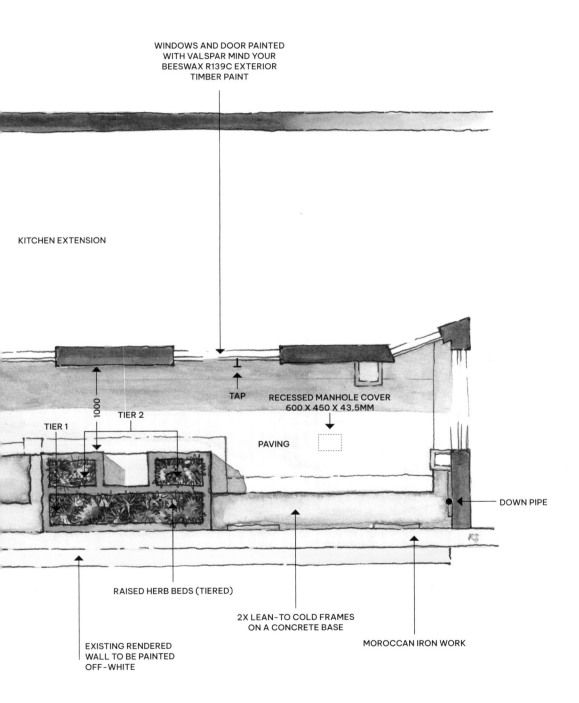

WINDOWS AND DOOR PAINTED
WITH VALSPAR MIND YOUR
BEESWAX R139C EXTERIOR
TIMBER PAINT

KITCHEN EXTENSION

1000

TAP

RECESSED MANHOLE COVER
600 X 450 X 43.5MM

TIER 1

TIER 2

PAVING

DOWN PIPE

RAISED HERB BEDS (TIERED)

2X LEAN-TO COLD FRAMES
ON A CONCRETE BASE

MOROCCAN IRON WORK

EXISTING RENDERED
WALL TO BE PAINTED
OFF-WHITE

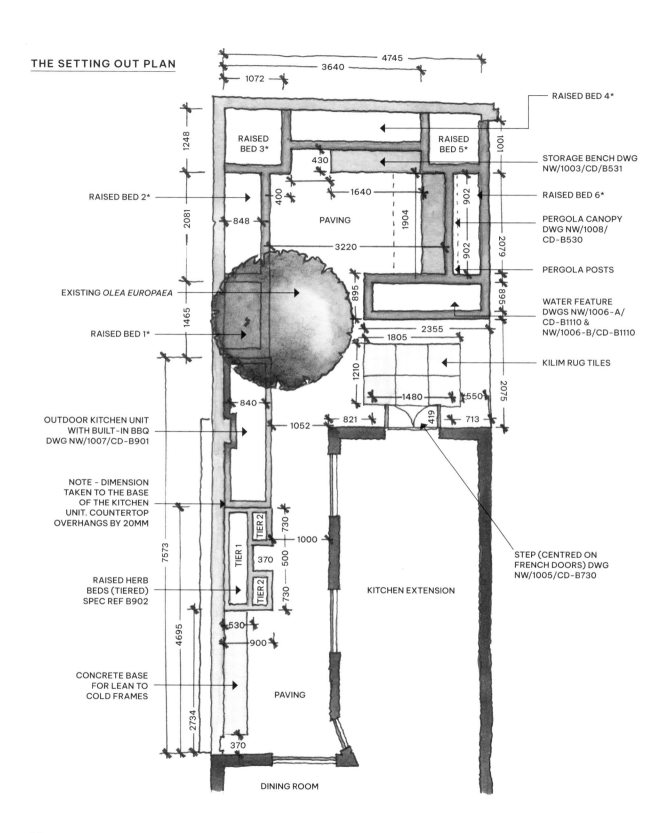

RAISED BED 4*

RAISED BED 3*

RAISED BED 5*

STORAGE BENCH DWG NW/1003/CD/B531

RAISED BED 2*

RAISED BED 6*

PAVING

PERGOLA CANOPY DWG NW/1008/CD-B530

PERGOLA POSTS

EXISTING *OLEA EUROPAEA*

WATER FEATURE DWGS NW/1006-A/CD-B1110 & NW/1006-B/CD-B1110

RAISED BED 1*

KILIM RUG TILES

OUTDOOR KITCHEN UNIT WITH BUILT-IN BBQ DWG NW/1007/CD-B901

NOTE - DIMENSION TAKEN TO THE BASE OF THE KITCHEN UNIT. COUNTERTOP OVERHANGS BY 20MM

TIER 2
TIER 1
TIER 2

STEP (CENTRED ON FRENCH DOORS) DWG NW/1005/CD-B730

RAISED HERB BEDS (TIERED) SPEC REF B902

KITCHEN EXTENSION

CONCRETE BASE FOR LEAN TO COLD FRAMES

PAVING

DINING ROOM

4745
3640
1072
1248
1001
430
902
1640
1904
400
848
2081
2079
895
3220
895
895
1465
2355
1805
1210
2075
840
1480
550
1052
821
419
713
7573
1000
370
500
730
4695
530
900
2734
370

Creating a setting out plan

Garden designers create setting out plans so that contractors have dimensions for all the different areas of the garden, which they will use to mark out the design on the ground. Use a copy of your unlabelled master plan to create this plan.

Where possible, keep as many of the measurements around the edge of the garden plan, exactly like labelling the master plan. Mark the length and width of the site.

Garden designers create setting out plans so that the landscape contractor has accurate measurements to refer to when marking out the design on the ground. For example, the length of a patio may run along the fence for 3m/10ft. This measurement is marked on the drawing. Then from the end of the patio the design may have a planting border 2m/7ft long. Again, mark it on. From the end of the planting border, there may or may not be any other design elements, so you mark the remaining measurement to the end of the rear fence. Breaking down the dimensions in this way is helpful for the landscape contractor to read the measurements and mark them on the ground. These measurements should be marked along the length and the width of the garden.

If you have curved lines or arcs, it is best to mark the central points and mark the radial measurements of the shapes.

Having completed your setting out plan, here comes the exciting part. Time to create your planting plan.

Creating a planting plan

Using another copy of your unlabelled master plan, you can now start creating your planting plan. Do this in pencil for now until you are totally happy with your plant choices and placements, and use your site analysis plan to check which plants will be happy where.

Start the planting plan by placing the structural plants on it, including trees and shrubs. Aesthetically, trees look much better when staggered through a border (avoid the back), with other planting weaving in and around them.

When choosing plants, first check their ultimate heights and spreads. This is especially important for trees and shrubs since some can grow huge and could potentially dwarf your space. Not only will they then look out of place, but they can upset neighbours by blocking their light. They may also prevent plants from growing around them. Once you know the spread of a tree, select the appropriate size of circle on your circle template and draw it on the plan with an H pencil in its preferred position. Do the same for all the trees and shrubs you want to include in your planting scheme. Mark the centre of each circle with a solid dot.

When you are happy with the placement of your structural plants, start populating the rest of the planting scheme.

Remember to create a hierarchy, placing taller plants at the back of the border and gradually working down to low-growing plants at the front. Also repeat the planting in the borders. For herbaceous perennials, ferns, grasses, and roses I tend to use a 40 or 50cm/15¾ or 19½in circle. These are usually planted in groups, so I draw the circles touching each other. For climbers I draw an elongated oval with a semi-circle protruding outwards from the centre. Another option is to draw an elongated triangle with the point facing out from the wall or fence. It is useful to see the balance of evergreens to deciduous plants within your planting plan. This way you can tell if you will have sufficient winter interest. Do this by filling all the evergreen plant circles with fine lines that are drawn at an angle.

If you find that you cannot fit all your plant labels on the page, I suggest labelling the borders as A, B, C, D and then re-drawing each border to scale on a separate piece of paper, with space around it for labels.

When you have populated your plan with all the plants, you are ready to ink it. Like the master plan, create different line weights using your micro-graphic pens. Ink the trees in 0.5, shrubs in 0.35 and plants that are lower than shrubs in 0.25. If you have groups of lower shrubs, small perennials, or ground cover, draw these also in 0.25.

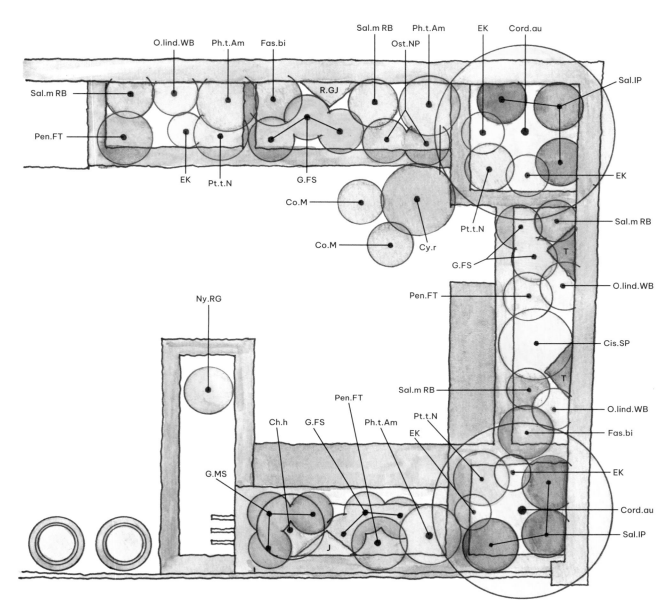

 J = JASMINUM OFFICINALE 'CLOTTED CREAM' X1

 G.MS = GERANIUM 'MAVIS SIMPSON' X3

 Pen.FT = PENNISETUM 'FAIRY TAILS' X3

 Pt.t.N = PITTOSPORUM TOBIRA 'NANUM' X3

 Fas.bi = FASICULARIA BICOLOR X2

 R.GJ = ROSA 'GERTRUDE JEKYLL' CLIMBER X1

 Ost.NP = OSTEOSPERMUM 'NAIROBI PURPLE' X2

 EK = ERIGERON KARVINSKIANUS X5

 Co.M = COREOPSIS VERTICILLATE 'MOONBEAM' X2

 Cis.SP = CISTUS X ARGENTUS 'SILVER PINK' X1

 T = TRACHELOSPERMUM JASMINOIDES X2

 Sal.m RB = SALVIA MICROPHYLLA 'ROYAL BUMBLE' X4

 O.lind.WB = OENOTHERA LINDHEIMERI 'WHIRLING BUTTERFLIES' X3

 Ch.h = CHAMAEROPS HUMILIS X1

 Cy.r = CYCAS REVOLUTA X1

Cord.au = CORDYLINE AUSTRALIS (MULTIHEAD) X2

 Sal.IP = SALVIA 'INDIGO PURPLE' X6

 G.FS = GEUM 'FIRE STORM' X8

 Ph.t.Am = PHLOMIS TUBEROSA 'AMAZONE' X3

 Ny.RG = NYMPHEA 'RENE GERARD' X1

Labelling plants

Plant names are always written in Latin, which is the international industry language. Therefore, a *Prunus lusitanica* is referred to by the same name throughout the world, no matter which country you are in, while the common name for this plant may differ from place to place, which could be confusing.

There are various ways that garden designers label plants. Some like to abbreviate the Latin names and create a key on the side. They will then mark on the plant circle the quantity of the plant x the abbreviation of the plant name. For example: 1 x Prlu, for one *Prunus lusitanica*. For groups of herbaceous perennials, follow the same steps. For instance, if you were placing three *Salvia nemorosa* 'Caradonna', write 3 x SalnemC. Other designers will write the quantity and the full Latin name around

the plan and extend a tag line from the label to the centre of one of the plant circles. Alternatively, you could use colours and create a colour key for each plant (a method best used for a small variety of plants). When you are happy with the position of the plants, you may want to ink your planting plan and apply touches of colour to it with some coloured pencils.

Creating planting elevations
To check the hierarchy of your planting scheme, make an elevation drawing from a base line that is your ground level. Then draw the plants to scale as if you were looking at them from the front, face on.

Creating a lighting plan

Creating a lighting plan helps you to decide which areas to illuminate and how you would like them to be lit. Are there areas that need lights for safety or practical reasons? Are there any trees you would like lit? Is there a focal point that needs illuminating? Can lights be used in fun ways for decorative purposes?

Lighting in a garden should be soft and moody, creating a warm, cosy ambience. I use different colour dots for different light fittings, placing them in the areas I want lit. To light the patio, you may want wall lights on either side of the door that leads from the house into the garden. You may also like some lights that are flush with the ground, so the beam skims the floor. Lighting steps, level changes, pathways and open water at ground level is also essential to make these features safe. In addition, I light up

trees and planting borders with discreet spike lights that provide a soft glow – placing some of them near a pathway can also offer enough illumination to light it too. Other elements of the garden you might think about lighting include screens, interesting wall textures, art, sculpture and water features.

Once you have placed your light symbols on your plan, you can choose which lights to connect on the same circuit. I do this by drawing a coloured line connecting the symbols for the lights I would like switched on at the same time. The circuit lines should all then lead back to the house. Once you have this plan ready and you have chosen your light fittings, sit down with a qualified electrician or garden lighting expert to go through the plan in detail.

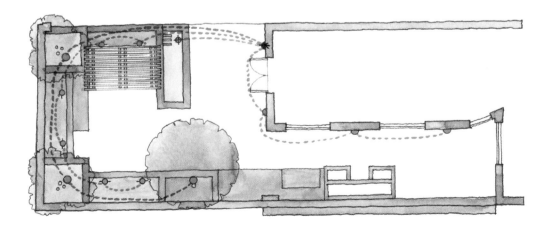

Garden design fundamentals

In this chapter I will guide you through
the fundamentals of designing a garden, from
patios and pathways to levels and lighting, with
inspirational ideas every step of the way.

When choosing materials, first and foremost
buy the best you can afford. After all, your
garden is an investment in your home and you
want your investment to last. While hardscape
materials can be expensive, they form the
backbone of any design, so take time to consider
which types will be best for your garden.
As well as the cost, it's worth considering
durability, maintenance and sustainability.

Select materials that are also going to stand the
test of time. Try to avoid going all out with a trend
that will be difficult to alter as fashions change.
Bear in mind that your hardscaped areas are the
backdrop to your planting scheme and should
play a secondary role to the plants.

Designing your social spaces

The design of the social spaces in your garden will depend on how you want to use them and with whom you will be sharing them. All too often homeowners keep their social spaces close to the house, but extending them further into the garden will give you a reason to venture from one place to another. Seating and dining areas then become destinations, connected by pathways that function as arteries through your garden, and give you more reason to explore and enjoy it.

How do I design the social spaces?

To answer this question, you must carefully consider how you want to use your garden?' There are two fundamental points that need to be answered:

− What type of activities will the garden be used for?
− Who will be involved in these activities?

Once you have answered these questions, you can then begin to design spaces that are fit for purpose.

For example, if you want to create a children's play area, you will want it at a distance where the young ones will not disturb an adult space but close enough for you to keep an eye on them. Or, if you want an area for a hot tub, you may need additional screening to protect you and your guests from prying eyes.

It is also important to integrate your social spaces into the garden as a whole, rather than designing them in isolation. Connect them using pathways, steps and level changes that lead from one area to the other. You can also define these routes with an arch, arbour, or several arches to create an interesting walkway.

Where do I position social spaces?

Most people like to keep their outdoor eating area close to the house. It is easier to bring the food and drinks out to the table and close enough if you need to nip back in to fetch something. However, if this means that you will be sitting on a cold, shady patio, you may want to create your eating area in a sunnier part of the garden.

It is also important to evaluate what times of the day you use the garden most and for what activities, which will help you to determine where your social spaces should be in the garden. For example, you could create a seating area for a relaxing gin and tonic after work in an area that receives the sun in the evening, or include a small area with a bench where two people can sit and have a chat over a cup of morning coffee.

Practical tips for social spaces
- Never position firepits under trees. There is a risk of the fire getting out of control. Always make sure the fire is out and cold when not being attended.
- It is always a good idea to keep young children's play areas in your line of sight.
- Think health and safety. Make the floor of your social space non-slip and ensure that any worksurfaces where you intend to cook or lay out food can be cleaned easily.

Choosing *materials*

Before we get into the specifics of social spaces, think about what hardscaping materials you want in your garden. Consider the following:

— The environment that your garden is in. Is it a rural, town or city setting?
— What materials are used in the surrounding homes and gardens?
— Consider colours and textures that will work sympathetically with the surroundings. However, this does not mean that you need to play safe.
— What colours, materials and textures have you used inside? Can you bring some of these outside to create that cohesion between indoors and outdoors?

You may want the colours, tones, or textures to match or work in total contrast to your home. However, using too many different materials creates division in a garden, so limit your choices to three. This will bring cohesion to your design and ensure the different areas work in harmony with each other.

What materials are available?

I love natural materials for their inherent characteristics such as the natural strata lines in stone and the grain in wood. I favour limestone which is highly durable and has a smoother finish than sandstone. My absolute favourite is jura limestone. It comes from the upper Bavarian region in Germany and includes fossilized leaves, twigs, insects, and other creatures ingrained within it. If you are very lucky, you may even get a slab featuring a perfectly formed ammonite.

MATERIAL CHOICES FOR DIFFERENT AREAS OF THE GARDEN INCLUDE:

Patios
Stone slabs; clay pavers; porcelain; preformed concrete slabs; timber or composite decking; stone or urbanite flags.

Pathways
Gravel; clay pavers; timber or composite decking; bricks; stone or urbanite flags; crushed concrete; stone setts; chipped bark.

Ordering materials
When looking at materials or any products for your garden, remember to ask the supplier about lead times for delivery. This information will help you to order goods in time and prevent delays, especially if items need to be sent from abroad.

Walls
Bricks; oak sleepers; concrete breeze blocks that can be finished with render or clad with tiles, porcelain, brick slips, timber, or metal sheeting; gabions filled with your choice of materials – try filling the backs of gabions with rubble, which cannot be seen, and use your good materials on the faces that are visible.

Steps
Weathered steel or sleeper edges with gravel backfill; preformed concrete steps; clay pavers; bricks; concrete formation with stone treads and risers can be clad with clay pavers; porcelain; metal.

Structures
Timber; willow; aluminium; bricks.

Designing your *patio*

What size do I make the patio?

When designing a patio or decking for dining, consider how many people will use the area. The answer will dictate the size of your furniture and the floor area needed to accommodate it. Also check that there will be enough space behind the seats for other people to pass by and for those seated to move their chairs back, away from the table. You do not want people to feel squashed and uncomfortable, or fall into your borders and destroy your beautiful plants.

What shape should I make the patio?

Give your patio an interesting look. Be creative and consider a curved, L-shaped or even a round patio, rather than the usual square or rectangle. You might also want to make your patio bigger so that you can incorporate some planting beds into the hardscaped area, thereby bringing the garden all the way up to the house. Or try setting your patio at a 45-degree angle to the house to create a more dynamic design. When designing curved lines and circles, bear in mind that these shapes will incur more material wastage, while cutting and installing them also requires some level of skill, which will increase the cost.

Tips for patio drainage

When laying a patio, it is important to make sure that surface water runs either into planting borders or a drain. To ensure water drains correctly, there must be a very gentle fall to the patio, the ratio of which will be determined by the material you use. Always ask your supplier about the fall ratio they recommend for your choice of materials.

What materials should I use?

The materials in your garden should reflect the theme you've chosen. If it's a contemporary garden, think about paving units with large dimensions, clean lines and smooth surfaces. Look at sawn stone, porcelain or preformed concrete slabs that will work seamlessly with a modern look. Porcelain tiles come in a variety of different finishes resembling wood, stone, and concrete. Alternatively, try smaller units such as setts and clay pavers laid in a contemporary pattern. Encaustic tiles with bold graphic patterns in a small area can really define a space too.

For a more traditional look, use tumbled or riven stone, perhaps in varying sizes. The natural characteristics of these finishes will add a sense of age and history to enhance the garden theme. Flagstones in different shapes and sizes can be laid as traditional crazy paving or you can use tumbled setts or clay pavers. Consider widening the gaps so you can fill them with gravel. This will enhance the look and permeability.

All hardscaped areas will require some level of maintenance and different natural stones vary in their porosity, while some may need to be sealed to prevent staining. Ask your supplier if your choices require this treatment and, if so, which sealant to use, as well as the best method to use. Ensure to undertake it on a calm, still day and in an area with no building dust in the air as it will stick onto the slabs whilst being sealed.

Permeable materials for hardscaping

A permeable hardscape surface allows rainwater to penetrate into the soil, thereby helping to prevent localized flooding, which can carry pollutants into waterways.

To make a patio or pathway permeable, choose natural materials. Solid stone with concrete foundations and pointing won't be permeable. However, there are new manufactured pointing and foundation materials that will allow water to permeate back into the ground. When ordering grout or bedding mortar, state that you want permeable materials. Or opt for a dry lay, where the slabs are laid on sand over an aggregate.

WHAT PERMEABLE MATERIALS CAN YOU USE?

Gravel is one of the cheapest permeable materials. You can use it for pathways, drives, as infills, and as a mulch. If you do not want the gravel to move around under foot too much, use the angular gravel (also known as chipped gravel). I prefer to use 10–14m/0.4–0.5in – anything larger will be uncomfortable to walk on.

Concrete can be recycled and used as a base for pathways to make them permeable. You can also buy permeable concrete slabs for your hardscaping, but other products made from this material and poured concrete foundations will prevent surface water from draining into the ground.

Urbanite is broken pieces of concrete, discarded from demolition sites. If you are willing to go and pick them up, you may get them for free. Urbanite can be used and laid in a similar way to flagstones or crazy paving, and the gaps in between filled with gravel or sand to make the surface permeable. Another option is to fill the gaps with low-growing planting or use small, round, washed pebbles to create a design in a few of the larger gaps. These will offer elements of surprise as you walk through the garden.

Pavers laid over a bed of sand or gravel is known as dry laying. This method allows water to pass through the gaps between each paver. You can also allow moss, grass, thyme or baby's tears (*Soleirolia soleirolii*) to grow in the gaps, which is a great way to breathe some life into hardscaping that may otherwise look quite harsh and sterile. Clay or brick pavers or stone setts can also be laid in this way.

Clay pavers are beautiful, and I love using them. However, to make sure the surface remains permeable, lay them on an unbound sub-base of crushed stone, slag or concrete, and fill the joints with free-draining aggregate such as sand or gravel.

Permeable resin-bound surfaces are normally used for driveways rather than garden paths or patios, although there are no rules stating that you cannot use them for such areas. They allow water to seep through the porous binder layer of coarse asphalt and then the sub-base layer, but do not mistake them for resin-bonded surfacing, which is non-permeable. Also remember that laying these surfaces is a skilled job, and it is worth employing a professional who knows what they are doing as this is a costly substance.

Permeable foundations

When looking at permeable foundations it is worth carrying out a percolation test to see how quickly your soil drains. Dig a hole 30 x 30 x 30cm/12 x 12 x 12 in. Remove all loose soil and stones. Saturate the hole with water and time how long it takes for the water to drain. If it is very slow to drain, consider an MOT type 3 sub-base rather than a type 1. Often used for the foundations of driveways, the size of material is larger than MOT type 1 and allows for better drainage.

Designing your *decking*

Where can I use decking?

Decking can be used for an outdoor social area. To determine the size and shape of the deck you need, use the same process as for a stone patio (see p. 66). Decking can be laid in a straight line or made to form a curved feature. You can also lay the timbers in different directions to make the feature look more interesting. The change in direction can signify a different use for that area, too. For example, a seating area can be laid in one direction and the dining space laid perpendicular to it, with each space defined by a deck border.

If you want your timber deck to last, position it in a sunny location which will dry quickly after rain or snow. A deck that remains wet or damp will eventually rot.

When to use professional skills

A word of caution. Whatever you are going to build in your garden, check your local building regulations before you start to make sure your plans are permissible. And if you are not skilled at building work, engage someone who is. Yes, it costs more money, but if your patio or wall starts falling apart, it will end up costing even more when drastic repairs are required.

What type of decking should I use?

Decks can be created in softwood, hardwood, or composite materials, and there are advantages and disadvantages to all of these. While timber decks can look lovely, they are not maintenance free and will need to be cleaned and oiled annually. Softwood decking is cheaper than hardwood, but the life expectancy is much less, while composite decks made from mixed materials may last as long as hardwood. Whether softwood or hard, timber decking generally comes with a smooth, planed face on one side and a grooved face on the other. My advice is to lay it with the smooth, planed face upper most. It may seem counterintuitive, but it will be less slippery, with fewer dirt deposits and less algae growth. Hardwood's durability means it is much more expensive, and products from both temperate and tropical forests can have a high carbon footprint. Softwoods grown in conifer forests in Europe are more eco-friendly and because the trees mature much quicker than hardwoods, they cost less too. Look out for softwood timbers that have been modified using a thermal process to make them more stable and durable, which gives them similar qualities to hardwood decking. Available from FSC-certified forests, this type of timber is also sustainable, has a low environmental impact and comes with a cost-effective price tag. Alternatively, if budget allows, you can use oak or chestnut decking (both hardwoods) from FSC-certified UK forests.

Sourcing sustainable timber

When using any timber in the garden, make sure it is sourced from a sustainably managed forest. It should be FSC-certified timber carrying the FSC (Forest Stewardship Council) stamp.

Designing *social* spaces without *hardscape*

∽∽∽∽∽∽∽∽∽∽∽∽∽∽∽

Social spaces needn't be constructed from hardscaped materials. If you want a more natural look with a lighter touch, consider mowing an area of lawn and include a bench, a pair of oak sleepers or even a couple of flat-faced stone boulders to sit on. You could also define the seating area by installing a planting border around it.

Another possibility is to create an area covered in gravel or chipped bark laid over a porous membrane, and defined with a metal or wooden edge and planting around it. Both methods create permeable surfaces that are kinder to the environment.

Designing *Pathways*

How do I design pathways?

No matter what your choice of material, one rule when designing a pathway is that it must lead somewhere. Pathways create a framework for movement within a space, connecting different areas and providing a transition from one space to another, be that a shed, bench, seating or a lounge area. Design your pathway so that it complements the look of your garden. Straight or angular paths work well in a formal design, while paths that curve will suit gardens with a more natural feel.

What materials can I use for paths?

When choosing materials for paths, make sure the style, colour and texture of those you select suit the look you are trying to create.

The simplest features are mown paths through longer grass or a meadow, or, if you have a garden with a woodland feel, consider a chipped bark path. Gravel would be perfect for a rural cottage feel, or if you want a path with a solid surface, choose any of the materials suggested for patios on pages 67–69. Using the same material throughout the garden will also create a cohesive look and make a small space feel bigger.

Can paths be more interesting?

The design of a pathway can impact the way you and your visitors move through the garden. Narrow pathways make people move quickly; wider paths create a calmer journey, hence people slow down their pace.

But paths are not just about getting from A to B. Remember the design and material choices of your path determine not only the direction but also how the user journeys along it. They can also influence people's mood and state of mind. A short journey along a straight path can be extended by adding a few twists and turns into the design, and those same twists and turns can also lead a person to stop and look at what you want them to see.

The paddle stone paths (tobi-ishi) that meander through Japanese gardens encourage you to concentrate. They slow you down, giving you time to contemplate and absorb your surroundings. Japanese timber plank paths constructed like narrow bridges and laid in zig-zag pattern have the same effect. They also have a more mystical function – the Japanese believe that evil spirits travel in straight lines so walking in zig-zag lines protects us from evil.

In Moorish and Paradise gardens the classic chahar bagh (four gardens) design divides the space into four, with rills or pathways leading out from a central water feature. The four paths (or rills) represent the four rivers of paradise, which are milk, honey, water and wine. Paradise gardens are all about our sensory experience, symbolism and how this connects us to God.

The design of a path can also evoke memories. Imagine a cottage garden path created from old setts and gravel mixed with some broken pieces of china. This adds time and history to the space, with echoes of past generations that have used that garden or memories of gardening with Nana.

While choosing materials that work with your garden's theme, also consider the users. For example, elderly visitors will need an even surface, while bark pathways might be a safer option for spaces used by very young children. No matter what type of pathways you design, they will all take you away from your everyday world into a space of a different order.

HERE ARE FIVE GARDEN THEMES WITH IDEAS FOR PATHS TO HELP INSPIRE YOU...

Contemporary garden

— Staggered planks laid as a path
  where plants soften the sides and
  some groundcover plants creep into
  the gaps between the timbers.
— Encaustic tile paths with
  bold graphics.
— A modern crazy paving path
  with sawn clean-cut flags laid in
  a random pattern. The pointing
  gaps can be filled with gravel or
  groundcover planting.

Cottage garden

— Old planks from seaside piers can be
  recycled and make a pathway for a
  coastal cottage garden.
— Sandstone setts used both as an
  edging along a gravel path and
  squares or diamond shapes within
  the path. Old chips of bricks and
  china mixed into the gravel lend the
  path a sense of time.
— Flagstones laid with large gaps to
  allow for a gravel infill and ground-
  cover planting. Get creative by laying
  a mosaic with pebbles within the
  larger gaps.

Japanese garden

— A raised path created from decking planks installed above the gravel to evoke a sense of crossing over water.

— Large, rounded paddle stones gently rising from the gravel (or moss) give a spiritual look.

— Long stone planks combined with pieces of broken stone in random sizes; offers a great opportunity to recycle old stone slabs.

Tips on non-slip surfaces

If you live in a cold, wet climate, select materials for paths and patios that are suitable for your garden environment. Tiles and slabs with highly polished surfaces will become slippery when wet or in snowy conditions. Exterior surface materials, whether for paths or patios, should have an R10 or R11 slippage rating, so confirm this with your supplier. Also check that materials are frost proof.

Moorish garden

— Lay two different colours of zellige tiles in zig-zag patterns, one colour row next to another. Zellige tiles are better suited to hot, dry climates as they are slippery. However, the same shape and colours are available as encaustic tiles.

— Use pebbles of different colours to create an intricately patterned path that resembles a kilim runner (rug).

— Lay clay or encaustic pavers in a classic herringbone pattern, or in zig-zag rows as for the zellige tiles, using two different colours.

Moroccan courtyard

— Use clay pavers laid in a herringbone pattern for both the patio and pathways.

— Lay encaustic tiles in a bold graphic pattern.

— Include tiles with the traditional multi-faceted star patterns that are often seen in Moroccan and Moorish gardens.

Working with *levels*

Where do I need steps?

Most people include steps in a garden for purely practical reasons, but they can also offer a world of design opportunities. A level change in a flat space can add depth and character while making a small garden feel bigger. A step up can lead to a private seating area made cosy with beautiful metal screens or planting. A step down could lead you to a sunken, secluded garden.

You can also use steps to lead to a focal point such as a sculpture, stunning container, or an arbour. If you create steps with enough depth, they could double as seating with the addition of a few cushions.

In a sloping garden, it makes sense to introduce steps and level changes to make your garden more usable. Employing a method of cut and fill, you can sculpt the land, creating areas for steps and using the soil that you remove to fill the space above to level it out. This method may also require retaining walls to hold the soil in position and prevent it from collapsing.

Step finishings

Modern step treads should have an overhang of approximately 3cm/1¼in from the riser. The tread edge that faces outermost can be finished in various ways, such as bullnose, half-bullnose, pencil edge, chamfered or down stand. It is also worth including a drip line under the overhang, which will prevent rainwater running down the risers and staining them.

How do I design garden steps?

Interior and exterior steps are very different. Interiors stairs are higher and narrower, and while they feel comfortable inside, it is a very different story outside. Outdoor steps should feel generous and comfortable. The risers should not exceed 15cm/6in and the tread depths should be at least 40cm/16in. The design of your steps will also depend on the terrain. However, I would avoid splitting the garden in half through the centre. Like the calmness and balance that symmetry evokes, there is something equally aesthetically pleasing to the human brain about groupings in odd numbers. Divide the garden into three sections on the horizontal plane. They do not need to be equal sizes but aesthetically this will make them more pleasing. Set the steps to one side, creating a landing at the next level. From the landing, create a walkway to the opposite side of the garden and position the next set of steps to the third level. This approach creates a longer journey and can make your garden feel bigger.

Steps can also be curved but remember that cutting curved lines requires skill which pushes the price up. If your garden has a natural, sustainable look, consider naturally flat stone boulders positioned into cut sections of the terrain. Or in a contemporary garden, I love to include a 'shadow gap' between each step. This is a small gap between the riser and the tread below that makes the steps look like they are floating.

What materials can I use for steps?

You can use the same materials for steps and level changes as for patios and pathways – just remember to choose those that work seamlessly with the theme of your garden.

If you are aiming for a modern look, try slick, smooth sawn surfaces. For the risers, options include bricks, clay pavers, natural walling or panelling stone, or even metal panels.

Steps can also be constructed in bricks or clay pavers, and you can create some very interesting lay patterns, too. Or, for an easy solution, consider preformed steps made from weathered steel or concrete. In a city garden, metal mesh treads underplanted with shade-loving plants such as ferns offer a stylish design option; the plants just pop through and along the sides of them.

For a rural cottage-style gardens, opt for natural materials. Sleepers can be used as risers and back-filled with gravel. Or try reclaimed bricks, clay pavers, natural walling or panelling stone for the risers, with natural stone treads such as Yorkstone or riven sandstone.

Using *screens*

〰️〰️〰️〰️〰️〰️〰️〰️〰️〰️〰️〰️

Screens to make a garden feel bigger

If you have a small garden, one of the best ways to make it feel bigger is to install some screens. By masking areas or guiding the direction of travel, they can create a sense of intrigue, discovery and arrival, tricking the brain into thinking the garden is larger than its actual size.

Planning regulations
Before adding tall features such as screens to your garden, consult your local planning regulations to check that they comply with the rules in your area.

Screens for privacy

When deciding where and what type of screen to install, first have a look around your garden. Think about where you want to sit and what currently overlooks the area before making your choices. Trees provide natural architecture and screening in a garden, delivering height, impact and privacy, and you may only need one, placed strategically to block the view from a neighbouring window. Trees also help to absorb pollution. If you have limited space and don't want to block out too much light, consider planting pleached trees along the boundary to create an aerial screen without breaching any planning regulations. And they will prevent inquisitive eyes from prying into your personal space. Box-head trees can also be used in the same way, but bear in mind these are expensive. Pleached and cube-head trees suit a modern garden, although you can also use standard trees with a spreading canopy to achieve a similar effect.

Tall hedges can also act as a screen to mask a neighbour's view, but make sure you keep them under control. You must not block out light from your neighbour's internal rooms or you may end up with a dispute on your hands.

Bamboo can be used as screening, too, but be aware that its spreading roots will run and can be invasive. To prevent this, use a root barrier around the root balls.

A timber trellis or cedar slats can be installed on top of a boundary wall to provide additional height for screening, and will block the view even more if greened up with climbers.

Screens for seating and hideaways

Rather than lining the whole boundary with pleached trees to create privacy, another option is to wrap trees around cosy seating areas and hideaways. The vertical trunks will create the feeling of a room, while the canopies provide a screen. The pleached trees can be underplanted with tall ornamental grasses. Alternatively make a screen of tall perennials and grasses of varying heights to surround yourself with colour and texture. Or create a natural pergola with seating underneath using umbrella trees, also known as rooftop trees. These are trained on a frame to form a flat, square canopy, giving cover from above.

Screens can also create secluded hideaways and areas designed for contemplation. Hedges are a good choice for these features, providing a sense of intrigue and discovery.

Screens for direction and focus

Hedges can also be used to direct your eyes to a focal point such as a stunning piece of sculpture, a beautiful pot or a specimen tree – a row of trees will create a similar effect in a larger garden.

Screens to hide unwanted views

If there are ugly features in the garden such as compost piles, refuse bins and sheds, or an unsightly view beyond the boundary, you may want to use a screen to hide them. Hedges will create a green wall to screen eyesores, or consider a tree with a spreading canopy to mask the view of a pylon or a phone mast in the distance. Check that your chosen tree will eventually grow to the height you need to cover what you wish to obscure.

Maintaining pleached and cube-head trees

Young pleached or cube-head trees are generally cheaper than mature ones, but their branches will need to be trained onto a bamboo or metal framework, which will take time and effort. Mature shaped trees also require annual maintenance. If you choose to have these professionally pruned and trained this does add to the cost. Many companies offer this service but it is expensive. An easier alternative is to plant normal standard trees or multi-stemmed trees and 'lift' the canopies, which is easily done by removing the lower branches to create long, clear trunks.

Other screening options

Trees and hedges are not the only screening options; here are some other alternatives to consider.

Arbours, arches and pergolas

These features may be constructed in timber, metal, or willow. Arbours and arches laden with climbers and vines not only provide screening, but can also act as gateway from one part of the garden to another. Pergolas can provide a secret seating area, where decorative metal screens or trellis covered with climbers have been fixed to the sides to create an enclosure.

Laser-cut screens

Metal screens made from weathered steel, powder-coated aluminium or a composite decorated with dramatic laser-cut patterns can be used as a stand-alone art installation, or to hide unsightly areas or provide privacy. These screens can also be incorporated as roof panels on a pergola, providing some shelter and screening from above. Light the screens from the back or above and they will cast magical patterns on the ground. Choose a pattern that has small cut-out shapes, as these will produce more defined shadows. Remember to select a pattern that works within the theme of your garden.

Using weathered steel

When using weathered steel (corten) products, bear in mind that they can cause staining, so it is best to position them on or against gravel so that any drips of stain drain into the gravel rather than ruining your beautiful stone. If using weathered steel sheeting as cladding, include either a drip gap between the cladding and the adjacent material or create a gravel strip between the two.

Willow screens

Natural woven willow screens are sustainable, look good, and are easy to replace if need be. You will require the artisan skills of a willow weaver to make a screen, so buy premade panels, or you could take the opportunity to learn a new craft to create your own. A quick way to make a willow arch is to plant living willow rods in the ground, which will then root in the soil and grow. When they are tall enough, you simply tie the stems into an arch at the top.

Slatted screens and trellis

Panels of cedar slatting lend themselves to both city and suburban gardens. They can be installed horizontally or vertically and used for fences, trellis on top of a boundary wall or as stand-alone screens to create a private seating area or to hide the shed or compost bins. Timber trellis panels can be used in the same way but they look best covered with climbers and vines, or you can train an espalier fruit tree on them.

Posts

Sometimes it's the simplest ideas that can work the best. A row of timber posts set with a small gap equidistance apart, creates a screen and a lovely backdrop for some beautiful planting. You could even char the posts or paint them a colour of your choice.

Alternative ideas for screens

An old, ornate metal gate or a carved timber door can be transformed into a screen that also makes a beautiful focal point in the garden. You can even train a climbing rose over the gate.

Another quick, easy and cost-effective idea is to use a reinforcement mesh panel as a screen. Secure it between two timber posts and grow your choice of climbers over it – evergreen climbers such as star jasmine (*Trachelospermum jasminoides*) or ivy (*Hedera helix*), will create a year-round hidden space. This will also hide unsightly features and divide the vegetable plot from the ornamental garden.

If you are going uber contemporary how about using Perspex panels? These come in beautiful colours and will look great at night when they are lit and you see silhouettes of planting and garden features behind them. Source Perspex from a sustainable supplier.

Installing posts

Cut the tops of your posts at a slight angle or a shape that allows rainwater to run off, which will prevent them from rotting. Also coat the section of the post that will be buried in the ground with butyl paint and wrap it in a waterproof membrane for additional protection. Hammer the posts into gravel-filled holes so that they do not end up sitting in wet soil.

Remember that all timber will fade to a silvery-grey colour as it's bleached by the sun, and you will need to stain it if you want to keep the original hue.

What should I do about my *boundaries*?

All properties and gardens have boundary lines, but always check which ones you are responsible for. This information is usually on the title deeds of your property. Most suburban gardens' boundary lines are fences, which planning regulations in the UK allow up to a maximum height of 2m/6½ft. If you live in a conservation area there may be other conditions regarding your boundaries, too, such as the materials or styles you can use. For example, in some areas of London only privet hedges are allowed.

Cedar or composite slatted fences work well in a contemporary setting, or, of course, you could opt for hedging to define the boundary. Providing instant green impact, hedges also create wildlife habitats, and capture pollution too. If you are living in a city, you may like to go for a closely clipped formal-looking hedge to suit the formal architecture of buildings so often found in cities. If you live in a suburban area where the architecture of properties is informal, you could choose either an evergreen hedge or deciduous beech or hornbeam and keep it less severely clipped so it has a more relaxed look. A native hedge grown from young whips of plants such as birch, hornbeam, hawthorn, blackthorn, hazel, dog rose, dogwood and alder would suit a rambling rural garden. There are various hedge themes to choose from such as flowering, bird-friendly, edible, and even a gin-maker's mix.

Alternatively, you could build a boundary wall. The most popular are brick walls but if you live in a rural setting you could use a local stone such as Purbeck or chipped flint. Cathedral sandstone or paddle stone walling can also convey that country cottage look. If you want a wall with an interesting texture for a contemporary garden, consider wild stone natural walling which comes in a variety of stones and can be used as cladding on a breeze block construction. If you have the patience, urbanite can also be cut down and used to build walls.

Making a garden feel *bigger*

I am often asked by clients if I can make their small garden feel bigger. There are some easy tricks that will help. You can create a journey by changing the direction of a path or introduce a level change. Reflections that trick the eyes, false entrances, hidden zones and borrowed landscapes will also help to make your garden feel larger. Even a balcony can feel more spacious if you keep the floor space clear, avoid too much clutter and use the vertical surfaces for planting. Wall mirrors can trick the eye into thinking the space is bigger, too. Or, if you want to be creative, how about painting a landscape mural on a wall or commissioning an artist to do this?

How do level changes work?

One of the simplest tricks in a small garden is to create a level change. A step up has created a journey, already making the garden feel a little bigger (see p.79). By adding some interesting things to look at en route, you slow the visitor down (see also page 74) and trick the brain into thinking the garden is a more generous size.

How can I use mirrors?

Using a mirror on the rear boundary is a great trick to make the garden feel bigger. It is important to have flowers, shrubs and trees reflecting in the mirror and use plants such as climbers or tall grasses to disguise the edges, too. Blurring the lines between the real plants and the reflection will give the impression the garden extends even further.

How do false entrances and screens work?

Adding a false door on a wall or fence, with a path leading to it, creates mystery. What is beyond that door? That simple question makes us feel the garden is bigger and there is more space to explore. Just make sure the door reflects the rest of your design.

In a small garden you can often see everything straight away, which makes the space feel even smaller, but by screening some areas, you can disguise the boundaries and add mystery and intrigue. This fools the brain into thinking the space is larger while enquiring minds will want to find out what is hidden behind them (see p.82 for more ideas).

How do I use diagonal design lines?

You do not have to limit your design to lines and shapes that run straight up and down the garden. Some of the most breathtaking gardens are designed on a diagonal – try positioning your grid or design at a 45 degree angle to the house and see how it looks. This technique can be particularly effective in wide, shallow plots where a diagonal line will give you the longest vista through the space.

A mistake that I often see is narrow planting strips along the perimeter of a small garden with open space in the middle. This prevents you from creating a dynamic scheme with repetition,

rhythm and layers of plants. Diagonal design lines will help you create deeper planting borders while also making hidden areas for seating, and the pathways will zig-zag through the space, creating a longer journey.

How can I 'borrow' the neighbouring gardens?

Garden designers will often talk about blurring the boundaries. If neighbouring gardens have trees and shrubs that are visible from your garden, make them part of your design and use plants in your space of a similar height, colour, form, or foliage shape to take the focus away from the boundary lines. If you cannot see where one garden ends and the other begins, you have successfully blurred the boundaries, making your space feel bigger. You can also do this with architecture. If you see a church steeple in the distance, think about reflecting its shape, perhaps using topiary or an obelisk planted with climbers in the borders.

How does repetition help?

In a small garden too many different materials, colours and plants can make the space feel cluttered, but limiting your palette and repeating plants and features can help to make your garden feel more spacious. Try using the same surface material in different areas, repeating one colour, or weaving the same plant through all the borders to unify the design.

Your Outdoor Room

Lighting

Why add lighting?

Lighting can bring your garden to life once the sun has gone down, and there's no better way to bring a totally new ambience to your outdoor space after dark. Even if your budget does not stretch to lighting the whole garden, at least do the first fix. This means installing cables, so that if they need to run under paving or paths, the work can be done while the building is taking place. Laying the cables gives you the opportunity to add the light fittings later if you need to do the work in stages.

Choose LED lights and check the IP (ingress protection) ratings for fittings and bulbs, which will tell you if they are suitable for gardens. The higher the IP rating, the more protection they have from the elements – I prefer to use those with an IP rating of at least 65 to 67. If you are not sure, discuss your lighting plan with your electrician or your electrical lighting supplier.

What type of lighting do I need?

As the day slowly draws to a close, beautiful lighting can create a magical ambience in your garden, helping to extend the time you can enjoy your outdoor space, while also making it safe. Ensure the light fittings that are on show work with your theme and aim for a subtle, warm glow, rather than a bright, brash effect. If you have beautiful trees in your garden with lovely bark and branch structure, use uplighters to make a statement. Uplighters will also show off walls with interesting textures, while up and down lights can bring the brickwork of house walls to life. Practical lighting can still look beautiful, too – spike spotlights in planting borders cast enough light on paths to make them safe to walk along after dark.

Positioning lights among plants can also cast stunning shadows that add drama to your garden at night, and water features look especially beautiful when lit underwater, particularly if the water is clear and moving gently. Adding spike lights around the edges of ponds also helps to keep everyone safe.

LED strip lights are very popular and add intrigue and depth to otherwise rudimentary elements of the garden. They can be used under the overhang of a step tread or decking, or under the tabletop of a bar or outdoor kitchen. If you have a balcony, use lanterns, fairy lights or festoon lights to bring a warm glow to your outdoor space.

WHAT LIGHTING METHODS CAN I USE?

— Uplighting is best used for illuminating tree canopies, highlighting the beauty of their shape and branch structure. Install the light fitting approximately 2–3m/7–10ft away and angled up towards the canopy.

— Downlighting can be used to illuminate seating areas, pathways, planting borders or even a focal point that you want to show off. Position the light fittings in trees and angled towards the area or object that you wish to highlight, or install wall-mounted downlights.

— There is nothing like the romance of moonlight. Mount a light fitting with low-voltage LED bulbs in a tall tree in your garden. The light will filter through the foliage and branches, illuminating the ground below and casting beautiful soft shadows. As the leaves move in the breeze, they will dance on the ground, evoking moonlight.

— You can create silhouettes of objects to add drama and mystery to the garden. Add a spreading light behind the object to show it in profile and create a silhouette.

— Throwing shadows onto walls or fences is something I particularly love. Plants or objects that are washed by light will create beautiful shadows on these surfaces.

— Pathways that run alongside planting borders can be efficiently lit with spike spotlights. For other pathways, use bollard lights or recessed lights – choose fittings designed to illuminate at 90°, 180° or 360°.

— Patios and decks can be illuminated with recessed lights. You can use walkover lights that sit completely flush with the surface, but the beam is directed upwards rather than across the surface, so they can be blinding when walking past them. To avoid this, install low-voltage lights or position them in out-of-the-way areas.

— To illuminate a textured surface, such as a wall, use angled spotlights on the ground that cast light across it. Up- and downlights can also be used, depending on the design of your wall and its position.

Can I have fun with lights?

The answer is definitely yes. Try these ideas for impromptu lighting when entertaining, and remember to never leave live flames unattended, and keep them away from trees, plants and children:

- Recycle jam jars: fill them with a little sand and place tea lights inside. These can be set on the table, along a path or hung from a tree using some galvanized wire.
- Tea lights also look effective when floating in a large glass bowl partly filled with water.
- Candles add a magical touch to any space. Use them in lanterns or storm jars and place them around your social spaces, or use different sizes of lantern in a group of three to create even more impact. Do not be afraid to elevate lanterns or storm jars onto a podium.
- Festoon lights provide a party atmosphere. You can run them in a zig-zag formation across an outdoor dining area or hang them around the framework of a pergola.
- Use fairy lights wrapped around an arch or moon gate to give these features an enchanted feel at night.
- Flames from a real firepit not only provide light but warmth, too, creating a cosy, intimate space.
- If space is limited, or you don't want to annoy the neighbours with smoke, choose a firepit fuelled by ethanol or granular gels.

- You could create the feel of a firepit by placing logs in a large metal dish and wrapping fairy lights around them.
- Look out for plant containers that light up at night to create a glow on your patio.
- Lights set into ornaments or features that look like stone boulders can be placed among your plants.
- Add swaying lights to your planting borders. These small light bulbs on flexible stems slot into the ground and sway in the breeze.

What are the benefits of solar lights?

Solar lights run on the energy from the sun, so the solar panels need to be placed in a sunny part of the garden. It is worth looking at the cost of solar lights and how long their life expectancy is. In fact, there are a number of elements to consider:

Pros
— They save on energy costs.
— They do not require cables and hard wiring.
— Solar lights are easy to install. They are normally spiked into the ground or screwed onto the wall.
— Solar lights do not require much maintenance, other than cleaning the solar panel regularly and changing the batteries every two to five years.

Cons
— Solar lights rely on prolonged exposure to the sun to generate energy.
— Lights need to be installed where the solar panels will get adequate sunlight.
— Lights are not as bright as electrical fixtures.

Light pollution
Light pollution is caused when our natural night-time environment is over-illuminated using artificial lights. The negative impact of this are:

— It drowns out the beautiful starlight in the night sky.
— It wastes energy .
— Disrupts the natural sleep and wake cycles of wildlife with daytime species becoming active at night, and not getting enough rest and sleep.
— This disruption then has a knock-on effect on their seasonal behaviour and reproduction.
— If wildlife activity changes, then this also disrupts the interactions between predatory wildlife and their prey.

To help reduce the effects of light pollution:

— Use light fittings that point the light down rather than upwards.
— Fit hoods on light fittings to reduce light pollution of the night sky.
— Use light fittings with eyelids.
— Choose fittings with frosted glass.
— Turn garden light off when not in use.
— Use PIR motion sensors where possible.
— Use lamps with gentle hues such as warm white, yellow or amber.

Creating a sustainable sanctuary

4

When designing your garden, think about it as your own personal sanctuary. Enhancing your garden with plants and water will encourage wildlife, bringing you closer to the natural world and benefitting your health and wellbeing. However, if you want to reap the rewards from your sanctuary, then with that comes some responsibility to the environment. It's worth spending some time thinking about the impact your garden has on the planet, and how you can make it as sustainable as possible. There is a vast amount of information out there on sustainability, ecology and biodiversity, so if you want to create an eco-friendly space, do a little research of your own and look through these simple tips, which will help to start you off on your design journey.

Why choose *sustainable* materials?

Whether it's for personal benefits, environmental benefits or helping out your community, incorporating sustainable design choices is much easier than you think. At the very least, knowing you are making the right choices by reducing waste will make you feel better about your actions and decisions. The positives for designing with sustainable materials are numerous:

— Sourcing locally often means you will be helping to support local businesses.

— By making sustainable choices today your actions are helping to protect the future of natural resources.

— Sourcing and using local materials will help to reduce your carbon footprint and you may pay less on delivery costs, too.

— Helping towards a greener planet through sustainable practice benefits our health by reducing the carbon released and preventing air pollution.

— Composting to produce your own organic soil conditioner will benefit your garden and save you money by reducing fertilizer use and its plastic packaging.

— Creating more planting spaces and minimizing hard landscaping will provide food and habitats for wildlife, including bees and other insects that pollinate many of our food crops.

— Reused or recycled items reduce waste that goes into landfill.

Recycle and upcycle

In our throwaway society, there is a real sense of achievement when you find a second-hand bargain or reuse an item and craft it into something new. And you will have saved a bit of money and helped the planet.

Salvaging and reusing

When creating a new garden, ask yourself if it is necessary to remove everything from it. Are there materials that can be salvaged and reused? Is there furniture that can be given a new lease of life by cleaning and painting it? Can old hardscape materials be lifted, cleaned and reused? Or is it possible to crush those materials to be recycled as hardcore for foundations? If your materials are in good condition and can be reused, salvage yards will take them away and may even offer you some money for them; they can also provide a great source for materials for your own project. I sourced an old millstone from a reclamation yard and turned it into a water feature for a client. A little tip – bricks bonded with cement mortar will be very difficult to clean and reuse, so look for those that have been used with lime mortar.

If you are into the shabby chic or Victorian-cottage look, the following ideas will be right up your street:

— Concrete slabs can be broken and recycled as crazy paving or kept whole and re-laid, with gaps between the pieces wide enough for a gravel infill and planting.
— Old roof tiles can be salvaged and reused, on end, as an edging.
— Clean, sand and reuse unwanted scaffold boards to make a bench seat or outdoor shelves for potted plants, or screw them together lengthways to create a wall. When painted, the wall can be used as a backdrop to a sculpture or beautiful planting.

— Use old zinc and galvanized buckets, containers, and basins as plant containers.
— Old chimney pots look great positioned among planting in borders. Plant them up with strawberry plants or trailing fuchsias. If you have three of different heights, group them together to make even more impact.
— 6mm/$\frac{1}{5}$in rebars can be easily bent into plant supports. They will rust and you will not even notice them among your plants.
— Empty wine bottles can create an interesting wall especially if it is then lit from behind. They can also be used as a face fill for gabions. You will either need to have a few parties or ask friends and family to collect their empties.
— Recycled bicycle spokes can be welded together to create an interesting screen, or used as a support for climbers.
— Old metal drums, oil containers and galvanized metal buckets can be recycled and repurposed as plant containers. Just clean them out and drill holes in the bottom for drainage.
— An assortment of different wooden chairs painted in your choice of colours can be used as seats around an old wooden table. Maybe refer to a bygone era for colours that build on your theme.
— An old iron gate can make an incredible focal point. If it is very ornately styled, show it off as is. If not, you can sand and clean it, then paint it in a lovely colour to draw the eye. Make sure you use a paint designed for metal.
— If you want an outdoor office, then why not recycle a shipping container? They

are solid, waterproof and well built. There are companies who will prepare and deliver them to you, but make sure there is sufficient access into your back garden.

— Old weathered planks could be repurposed for decking. Look for companies that specialize in recycled timber. If you are a dab hand at DIY then you could use the planks to create your own outdoor furniture; start with a simple bench if you are a novice.

— Recycle old sleepers for border edging or use them to construct raised beds. Do not use sleepers that have been treated with creosote – it is poisonous and will contaminate your soil.

— If you are thinking about building a brick wall, look at using reclaimed bricks to keep your carbon footprint low.

— Repurpose an old, felled tree into an organic-shaped seat or bench.

— The base and trunk of old uprooted trees can be used to create stumperies in shady areas of the garden with a selection of ferns and other shade-loving plants.

Sourcing through social media

Take advantage of your local social media websites – some offer construction materials left over from building projects. And do not be too shy to post a request on these pages – you never know who may have exactly what you are looking for. There are also various freecycling pages online, so check these pages, too.

Introducing *water*

Why consider water in the garden?

I know when I am near the sea or a lake and I hear the gentle sound of moving water, all the stresses of life wash away. Just looking at the clouds reflecting in still water helps to bring my blood pressure down and adding it to your garden will deliver a similar sense of calm. If you have ever been to the RHS Chelsea Flower Show, you will have noticed that water appears in nearly every garden, be it a cascading waterfall, trickling rivulet, or a simple reflective pool. It is an essential part of any natural environment and a lovely way to make any space feel more like a sanctuary.

Consider why you want water in your garden:

— Do you want it to create a sensory experience? Water can be cooling and soothing to touch on a hot summer's day – you might enjoy dangling your toes in a pond.
— Do you enjoy the calming effects on your senses when you hear moving water? The soothing sound can distract you and transport you to another place.
— The sound of moving water can also be used to drown out background noise.
— If you like aquatic plants then water in the garden is a must.
— Water is the perfect invitation for wildlife. Depending on the design of your water feature, birds, bees, butterflies, frogs, newts, hoverflies, damselflies and possibly even bats will pay a visit.

Choosing materials

Make sure that the look and the materials of your water feature work with the theme of your garden.

— A corten trough filled with water that has been dyed using hydra black liquid dye will make it look like a mirror. The clouds in the sky will reflect on the surface and the dark water also helps to prevent algae by screening the sunlight it needs to grow.

— If space is at a premium and you just want a small feature to grow some aquatic plants, try a large glazed pot. Plug the hole at the bottom with some sealant and, once set, fill the pot with water. Then add small aquatic plants of your choice. Do check that they will not grow too big.

— A half whisky barrel is another good option for small spaces. Fill it with water and don't worry if it leaks at first; as the timber swells the gaps will close and make it watertight. You can then place your aquatic plants in it. If you add fish, submerge a pump and filter, too.

— To build a small pond, either line it with a butyl rubber liner or use a preformed pond liner. You will require a pump and filter if you are going to include fish and plants. The capacity of the pump and filter needed will be determined by the size of your pond.

— An old millstone or a monolith water feature would be perfect for a Japanese-style garden. Both must sit on top of a sump covered with a strong metal grille to support the weight – disguise the grille with pebbles. Place a pump in the sump to move the water up through the stone and out over the edge; it will then flow back down into the sump.

Children and Water
A word of caution. If you have children, please be aware that a child can drown in 6cm/2½in of water. Choose or design water features wisely to keep your young ones safe.

Low-budget ideas

If you have the budget, then commissioning a bespoke water feature is a great idea, but if your money won't stretch to that, you could make your own, using the ideas on page 110. The other option is to buy a preformed water features off the shelf. These ready-to-use features may include a pump and filter and the styles include:

- **Metal or stone spheres** where the water gurgles through the centre. These sit on a sump, with a metal grille on top which you can cover with pebbles.

- **Water walls** are ideal for modern gardens and come in several different designs and materials, including chrome, weathered steel, glass and polyresin.

- **Infinity water tables** make beautiful contemporary water features. These are available in square, rectangular or circular shapes and come in weathered steel or powder-coated aluminium in a range of colours.

- **Wall-mounted water features** are a great idea where floor space is limited. Many have heritage styling and beautiful modern features.

Water for your plants

Any new garden will require some new plants and these will all need water to establish. Plants nutrients are absorbed in a solution of water, too. However, we also know that water is a precious and limited resource, and as our summers become increasingly hotter and drier and supplies become scarce, we need to use it wisely. So, what can we do? Here are some excellent ideas:

— Save rainwater that runs off the roof into water butts. It is easy to connect a drainpipe to a water butt with a converter kit. If you have room, you can connect up a couple of butts to each other, or choose a slimline model where space is tight.

— When choosing plants, use those that are drought tolerant and will need little or no extra watering once established.

— If your soil is very free draining, improve its water-retention capacity by adding mulches of organic matter (see p.43).

— Once new plants are in, water them well and then spread a 5–7cm/ 2–3in depth of mulch over the top of the soil. Bare soil loses moisture through evaporation and mulches help to minimize this while also suppressing weeds.

— Keep up with your weeding –weeds compete with your plants for water and nutrients.

— Water the soil around your plants so it goes straight to the roots, and avoid using sprinklers, which are wasteful.

— Do not water your plants during the hottest part of the day.

— Subsidise your watering with grey water from the bath or kitchen for ornamental flowering plants (though not fruit and vegetables).

— If you install an irrigation system use a leaky hose that sits directly on top of the soil, so the water filters directly down to the roots and there is less evaporation.

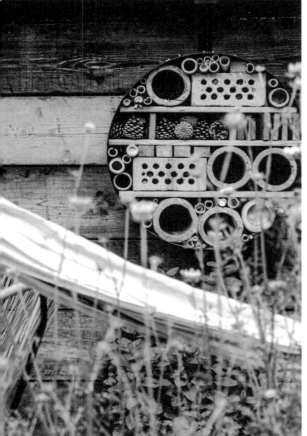

Homes for pollinators

Bees and other insects help to pollinate our ornamental plants and our food crops so they are great for the veggie patch and fruit trees. Our bee populations are declining so you could help reverse this trend by including a beehive in your design, or install a simple home for solitary bees. Choose from the beautiful products for solitary bees, such as bricks designed with just the right sized holes for them – simply replace the bricks in a boundary wall with them. Or you can make a bug hotel for your garden and place the brick in it (see p.117).

Habitat for wildlife

If you create the right conditions in your garden for wildlife, it will come. Hedgehogs are ground-dwelling creatures and in the wild they live close to woodlands, so hedges, shrubs and tall grasses are perfect for them. Hedgehogs help us, too, since they feed on slugs, snails, beetles, decaying organisms and other invertebrates. You can also encourage them by creating piles of fallen leaves, twigs and small branches where they can hibernate over winter.

Leave a pile of logs in a hidden corner of the garden, too. They make perfect hiding places for insects that will then attract frogs, hedgehogs and birds which feast on them. Log piles also support a range of plants and wildlife, from moss and fungi to insects and other invertebrates, reptiles and amphibians. As the wood decomposes the nutrients in the logs are released. The fungi and insects are the decomposers and consume the nutrients at an earlier stage, which they then release. These are recycled back into the soil where they are taken up by plants and other organisms. Water in the garden will also attract wildlife, from birds and bees to frogs, newts, bats, dragonflies and damselflies.

If you are keen on bats, you could also consider installing a bat box in the garden. Mount it between 3–6m/10–20ft above the ground and facing east or south, as bat boxes should have six to eight hours of direct sunlight per day in summer.

How do I invite birds into the garden?

Trees and hedges provide good habitats and the materials for birds to build their nests. Leave lint from your tumble dryer in the garden when birds are nesting, and they will use it to line their homes. I find in my own garden when I chop down the ornamental grasses, the birds will come and collect the dead leaves for their nests.

Also introduce berries and other plants that provide nourishment for birds, and feed the birds in winter when food is scarce, but reduce supplies when the weather warms up as you want them to help you control pests in the garden when they are more abundant.

You can also put up a birdbox. Site the box to face between north and east so that it does not overheat and is not exposed to the wettest windy weather. Also make sure that birds have a clear flight path in and out.

If you fancy being a bit quirky, nail an old work boot upside down on a tree and watch small birds convert it into a home.

I have a Cretan clay bottle hung on the wall in my garden in Crete and every spring the birds come and nest inside it. We love watching them flying in and out and listening to the chirping sounds of the young chicks.

Bug hotels

You can buy a bug hotel, but it's more fun to make your own. These structures are good for a variety of invertebrates, from ladybirds, lacewings and bees to beetles, spiders and woodlice. If you make them large enough, you could even include a hedgehog box at the bottom, and remember to include your hotel in your design plan.

The best time to start making and installing bug hotels is in autumn when insects are beginning to go into hibernation. They will provide a safe refuge, shelter and a place for them to lay eggs.

You can recycle old wooden pallets and planks of wood to construct your bug hotel; just make sure the ground is level so it won't fall over. You can include strips of wood, straw, moss, dry leaves, old terracotta pots, roof tiles, bricks with holes, logs, bark, pinecones, hollow bamboo canes, corrugated cardboard and dead hollow stems. Create cool, moist spots and warm sunny areas for bees. You can also look at the information online on how to build different styles of bug hotel. Investigate and have fun.

Designing a biodiverse garden

Biodiversity is the different kinds of life forms that inhabit one area, and includes animals, plants and microorganisms such as fungi and bacteria. All these species work together in harmony to create a balanced ecosystem.

Hindus believe in reincarnation and the circle of life, where everything on Earth is connected. We come from nature, and we go back to nature. Disturb or damage one part of that circle and it has negative effects through all the links that hold it together. In this way, wildlife and biodiversity work hand in hand. Increasing the biodiversity in your garden is a good way to protect all these forms of life and can be done without affecting the way you want to use your space or how you want it to look.

Benefits of biodiversity

Creating biodiversity in your garden will invite beneficial wildlife that will feed on the pests you do not want, reducing the need for artificial bug sprays that can harm all insects – the good as well as bad. When designing your garden, use these ideas to increase its biodiversity:

— When designing your planting scheme, include a range of plants that will be beneficial to wildlife. These can be rich in pollen and nectar and produce wonderful seedheads, hips and berries for wildlife to feast on.

— Introduce water in the garden, even if it is just a wide bowl that the birds, bees and other wildlife can drink from. I have two bowls in my garden which I keep topped up with water, and my mum loves watching the birds drinking and bathing.

— Leave an area unkept, perhaps hidden by a shed, where you might include a pile of logs and let weeds grow. Remember weeds are just plants in the wrong place and many also feed bees.

Planting for biodiversity

One of the best ways to increase biodiversity in the garden is to design a scheme with plants that benefit wildlife. Pollinators do not like hybridized plants that produce blooms with lots of petals that make it difficult for them to reach the nectar. Instead, choose open, single blooms such as asters, cosmos, achilleas, heleniums, rudbeckias and helianthus, and look out for other plants labelled with a bee symbol. Just including a few that are rich in nectar and pollen will create a biodiverse environment and produce lovely flowers, so everyone wins.

Growing plants that produce hips, seeds and berries will bring birds into your garden. Single-bloom roses such as *Rosa rugosa* and *R. canina* are good choices for hips. *Amelanchier lamarckii* makes a beautiful small multi-stemmed tree or shrub and also produces berries, while *Pyracantha coccinea* is an excellent wall shrub, providing winter interest with its red berries. Some birds may even build their nest in it.

Children love growing sunflowers, the seedheads of which will provide food for the birds in the autumn. The seeds of *Eryngium* and *Echinops* will also help to feed birds.

Planting trees and hedges also helps to create a biodiverse garden by providing a habitat and materials for nesting birds.

Water in a biodiverse garden

Introducing water into your design will attract wildlife and even a tiny feature will help bees and small birds. Make sure the water level is topped up so they can reach it.

If you have the space, think about a pond (see p.110) to attract frogs, newts, birds, dragonflies, damselflies and other creatures. When designing a pond, create a sloping beach-like side, and platforms or ledges to allow creatures to get in and out of the water easily and safely.

Can my balcony be biodiverse?

In a small garden or on a balcony, use the vertical space to grow a few wildlife-friendly plants that will increase biodiversity. I designed two small living walls on a roof terrace and the clients are delighted that Mr and Mrs Robin have built a nest and had their small brood in one of the panels. You can also include a small bowl of water for bees or butterflies and maybe hang a home for solitary bees on the wall.

A more *sustainable* approach

Sustainable practices in gardening can benefit both our own wellbeing and the environment in many ways. They can be more economical, too, often using recycled materials and reducing the impact on natural resources, while including plant-based materials such as willow for fencing, edging or screens that are biodegradable and can be replenished easily. Sustainable gardens may also require less maintenance, giving you more time to enjoy your outdoor space.

What is sustainability?

There are various categories of sustainability. In relation to our gardens, we are looking at environmental sustainability. Observing the relationship between the environment, wildlife and the nomadic tribes who live on the savannahs of Kenya, I noticed the latter take what they need, never more. It is like a spiritual way of living.

Simply put, sustainability is managing the needs and requirements of the present generations without depleting the resources that compromise the needs and requirements of future generations.

What does a sustainable garden look like?

A sustainable garden is beneficial to its surroundings, rather than having a negative impact. Allow me to paint a picture for you. Imagine stepping out of your home into your garden. You are greeted by scented plants that climb the walls of your house, with shrubs, grasses and perennials undulating at different heights in the beds below. Natural reclaimed material has been used to construct the patio. The rainwater drains away from the house into the planting borders. Recycled oil drums have been cleaned and painted with beautiful patterns, and used as containers both on the patio and within the planting borders as focal points.

The planting scheme is designed to create wildlife habitats and increase biodiversity with nectar-rich, berry and seed-producing plants. The planting is layered from the upper canopy of trees to shrubs, smaller shrubs, perennials and grasses, down to low-level planting and finally ground cover. This layering intercepts and slows down rainfall, helping to prevent flooding while capturing carbon dioxide and other pollutants, thus cleaning the air.

Old flag stones weave through the planting, creating a journey, while the spaces between them are filled with gravel and low-growing plants.

The pathway leads to a secluded seating area. Privacy is created with woven willow screens, and upcycled furniture sits under a tree canopy. These blend the garden with the views beyond. A hidden workshop/shed to one side is constructed from recycled corrugated roofing sheets, old scaffold boards and ethically sourced timber.

The borders are finished with a gravel mulch, reducing moisture loss and helping to keep weeding to a minimum. All green waste is composted. No chemicals are used in the garden. Organic forms of pest controls and natural predators help to keep unwanted pests and diseases at bay.

If you prefer a contemporary look, apply similar principles but choose materials with smoother, polished finishes and incorporate cleaner lines into the design.

I think you get the picture...

Creating a sustainable sanctuary

Easy ways to make your garden more sustainable

Making your garden sustainable is a step-by-step process. Start by making small changes such as those outlined below:

Beware plastic

Let's start with plastic. The black plastic pots that you may buy plants in at the nursery are non-recyclable and will most likely go into landfill, where they will take a very long time to break down. However, nurseries are adapting and the taupe-coloured pots many now use are recyclable. Some companies also recycle old pots, so return yours for reuse if your local store offers this service. Also avoid plastic trays to carry your plants home, and look out for pots and seed trays made from bamboo or a biodegradable composite containing rice husks. We do not want to put the nurseries out of business but what about propagating and doing plant swaps with like-minded gardeners? This is a good excuse to join a gardening group or club. The gardening community is very generous with plants and free advice.

Also invest in good-quality, non-plastic tools and a metal watering can, and look for second-hand tools and equipment online.

Lawns and alternatives

My clients often think that lawns offer an easy maintenance design solution, but this is not the case. The quintessential English lawn with perfect stripes takes a lot of hard work to achieve. In a shady garden, keeping a lawn looking good or even alive is even more difficult, so think about how much you need one and perhaps consider the alternatives.

Firstly, I am not an advocate of artificial grass, which is damaging to the environment and not good for wildlife. While some suppliers may claim that it is made from recycled materials, it is still plastic and the rubber backing takes years to break down. Artificial grass also has a big carbon footprint from its manufacture, through to transportation and installation. If not installed correctly weeds will grow through it and, contrary to popular belief, it will need maintenance such as cleaning and brushing. Unlike real grass, it is not pleasant to walk on, either, especially when it gets hot.

LET'S CONSIDER SOME ALTERNATIVES

- If you have children, what about play bark? If laid on a porous liner, it will allow rainwater to permeate through into the ground.
- Meadow turf is a great alternative. You do not have to worry about mowing and the flowers provide pops of colour and food for wildlife.
- In a damp, shady garden, consider a moss lawn (see centre right). It has a lovely velvety texture and is cushiony underfoot.
- Clover lawns (see top right) are worth a try. Just be aware that clover can creep into borders, so it does require some maintenance, although creating a deep edge along the borders could help.

- Gravel is permeable and allows for pockets of planting. I use 10–14m/0.4– 0.5in gravel which knits together well and is comfortable to walk on. Lay it on a biodegradable porous membrane to prevent weeds from coming up through the gravel.
- *Soleirolia soleirolii*, commonly known as mind-your-own-business or baby's tears, is a mat-forming evergreen. It grows rapidly, covering the soil surface and has a naturally mounding, creeping habit but may also invade your borders (see clover).
- Thyme is a good choice for free-draining soils. Corsican thyme releases a zesty fragrance when trodden on, while creeping thyme produces clouds

of tiny flowers that attract pollinators. However, note that thymes do not withstand heavy footfall.

— Chamomile lawns (see top left) work best where foot traffic is low. Easy to maintain, they require no mowing, feeding, fertilizing, or much watering (unless there are prolonged dry periods), and they release a sweet, fruity scent.

— A sedum lawn (see bottom right) will be drought tolerant and the plants' nectar-rich flowers are a magnet for pollinators.

— If you still want a lawn, use a creeping fescue grass to create an easy-care, close-knit sward.

Recycle green waste for compost

Rather than using artificial fertilizers and manufactured soil conditioners, you can enrich your soil with home-made organic compost. This will also save you money and reduce your use of plastic packing. Most garden soils have enough nutrients for good plant growth, so fertilizers are not generally necessary. Organic matter such as compost helps to make the nutrients in your soil more readily available to plants, while the overuse of chemical fertilizers can harm wildlife and pollute the groundwater which then runs into rivers, seas, and oceans, causing harm to the environment.

In autumn, rather than spending hours raking up all the leaves and disposing of them in plastic bin bags, leave them on your planting borders. Save yourself time and let the worms drag the leaves into the ground where they will break down. If you prefer to remove them, collect them in hessian sacks and leave them in a corner of the garden to decompose. You will be rewarded with wonderful leaf mould the following year. Plan spaces for compost bins, water butts and leaf sacks into your design, which will make them much easier to use and maintain.

When filling your compost bin try to create a balance of carbon- and nitrogen-rich items. For carbon, add shredded paper, cardboard, woody prunings and dried leaves. Grass clippings, kitchen vegetable waste and manure is rich in nitrogen. Do not put in cooked food as this will attract vermin and it is best to avoid citrus peel as the worms don't like it. Too many grass clippings can make the compost bin

very smelly, but adding shredded paper or card will absorb the excess moisture and help to reduce the odour. When we started our compost bin we also put in some worms, which help to break down the materials.

You can also add eggshells, nutshells, coffee grounds, tea bags (non-plastic), fruit and vegetable peel, kitchen scraps, stalks, cobs, toilet paper cores, sawdust, hay or straw, leaves, vacuum dust, natural fibres such as wool, hair, linen, cotton, hemp, unbleached paper towels, plant matter, spent flowers, paper bags, lint and egg cartons (cardboard). Do not add bleached or laminated paper, materials sprayed with pesticides, logs, cat litter, meat, fish, bones, dairy products, grease and oil, or large amounts of timber, coal, ash, or compostable plastic.

From time to time, you will need to turn the contents of your bin to add air into the mix. This helps to speed up the composting process. The compost must also be moist so do not let it dry out. If necessary, add some water to the bin. You can also apply accelerants to speed up the decomposition process.

It can take anything from six months to two years for garden compost to mature and be ready to spread on your borders. Mature compost is dark brown, has a crumbly texture and woodland smell. Spread your compost in spring as the ground is warming up but before all your plants have started shooting up through the soil. Any elements that have not broken down can be left in the bin for the next round.

The organic compost will reward you with a spectacular show and lots of strong growth and colourful blooms.

If you don't have room for large compost bins, you can purchase organic compost but avoid products containing peat. Peatlands absorb and store large volumes of carbon so you can help to tackle climate change by making sure you only use peat-free.

Machinery choices

We have all got used to using electric and petrol-powered machinery in our gardens that have a high carbon footprint. Petrol fumes add to air pollution, and while battery-powered tools might be a better choice, they are expensive. Perhaps, instead, you could consider some hand tools. These will save on energy bills and give you a good workout. I find clipping and shaping a hedge or shrub quite a creative and therapeutic process, too. It's also a fun way to get children involved.

Sustainable materials for hardscape

When choosing materials for hardscaping, think about where they come from and their carbon footprint. Sourcing and using local materials will have a reduced impact on the environment and delivery costs will also be lower.

5

Plants make a garden

Plants breathe life into an outdoor space.
They add colour and vibrancy to a garden,
making it feel warm and inviting. Conversely, a
garden with lots of hard landscaping, a lawn and
nothing else, or a front garden that is completely
paved over will look sterile and does little for our
wellbeing. When I first came to live in the UK in
1973, almost every house had a front garden.

They made homes feel welcoming and added
a sense of pride and community spirit.
There was even a bit of friendly competition
among neighbours. A space brimming with
flowers and colour is a good reason for passers-
by to stop, admire and have a conversation, and
highlights how plants play an essential role in
both our mental and physical health.

Choosing your plants

For most people choosing plants for their garden is the hardest part of the design. Many go to the nursery with enthusiasm, select plants that they like the look of without checking that they are right for their garden conditions, and then wonder why they fail to establish. While even an experienced gardener can expect a five per cent plant failure rate, a little knowledge and understanding will increase your chances of success and help you to create a beautiful planting scheme.

When does a yard become a garden? I created my first show garden 'Beneath a Mexican Sky' at the RHS Chelsea Flower Show in 2017, and the defining moment that I will never forget was when the first tree was planted. It immediately transformed what looked like a building site into a garden. Even now, with every design I set out and plant, I still have this same experience. For me, it is people that bring life into a home but it is plants that bring life into a garden.

Purchasing Plants

Plants are not cheap so here are some tips to consider when buying them.

- First, purchase plants from a well-established nursery that employs staff with plant knowledge who can offer you advice, and offers a stock of healthy plants.
- Look out for the cup symbol on labels, which signifies that a plant has the Royal Horticultural Society's Award of Garden Merit (AGM) and should perform reliably in your garden.
- If you are on a budget, spend money on structural plants such as trees and shrubs. Perennials, grasses, and ferns can come later.
- Buy young trees. They will be cheaper, settle in and establish quickly, and need less water than large established trees. Plus, you will get the satisfaction of watching them grow. The same is true for shrubs.
- When buying herbaceous perennials, those in 9cm or 1 litre pots may be cheaper but I tend to buy plants in 2 litre pots because they are more established and widely available. Another option is to buy a 5 litre pot and divide the plant into three if you feel confident to split it.

- The gardening community is very generous. Join a gardening club and you will soon find people will be offering you free plants.
- Sowing annual plant seeds is a great cost-effective way to fill the garden while you save up for longer-term plants.
- Before buying, knock the plant out of its pot to see if it has a well-established root system. Do not buy plants if the congested roots are circling around the pot or it has recently been transplanted and the roots have not established.
- Avoid plants showing signs of disease or blight, and those with nibbled leaves.
- If tree trunks have bulbous nodules on them ask if it is canker. Also look out for any other damage to the trunks or branches.

Taking inspiration from nature

A good way to understanding how plants grow is to take a walk in the woods. Here, the pioneer trees such as birches and rowans grow first and quickly create a protective canopy that allows the taller forest trees to develop. Once these begin to establish, other layers of plants follow. Next come the shrubs and climbers, followed by sub-shrubs and layers of ferns, grasses and perennials, as well as ground-covering plants that carpet the forest floor. Each plant layer affects those above and below them. Understanding the hierarchy of how plants grow in nature will give you a better understanding of where plants need to be placed in your garden. For example, you can plant daffodil bulbs under the canopy of a deciduous tree. These will bloom beneath the bare branches and die down as the tree's new foliage unfurls. You can apply this knowledge to your planting plan.

How do I assess climate, soil and sun?

When clients tell me about plants that have died in their gardens, it is usually because they have put the wrong plant in the wrong place. Understanding the conditions your garden offers will help you to make suitable plant selections. Therefore, at the beginning of the planning process, conduct a site analysis to identify your soil type (see pp.42–43), and areas of sun and shade (see pp.41–42).

Also check your regional and specific garden climate. If you live near the coast your garden will experience wind and salt spray. A garden on top of a hill is likely to be windy, while one at the bottom may be cold and frosty. In the UK where I live, we are lucky to live in a temperate climate. Despite being a relatively small landmass, as an island the climate is determined by the oceanic influences and varies from one region to the next. For example, the west coast is significantly warmer and wetter than the east in winter due to the heat capacity of the Atlantic Ocean and the Gulf Stream, while the east coast has a drier climate, with the warmest weather in summer in the south-east.

Choosing the right tree for your garden

Trees fall into two categories: deciduous and evergreen. You can select deciduous trees as standards, with a single trunk and canopy at the top, or as multi-stems, which have at least three main stems with the other branches growing from them. Most evergreens are sold with a single stem. If they are sold as multi-stem, they tend to resemble a tall evergreen shrub. When selecting trees for your garden check their eventual heights and canopy spreads and consider how much shade they will cast. Also remember that they absorb lots of moisture and nutrients, making it difficult for many plants to grow around them.

When selecting trees, consider these questions:

— Does it keep its leaves in winter?
— If not, does it have an interesting branch structure to enjoy after the leaves fall?
— Does it produce flowers and, if so, when?
— Are the flowers or foliage scented?
— Does it produce berries?
— Will it produce cones or catkins?
— Does it have lovely autumn colour?
— Does it have interesting bark textures or patterns?
— Which qualities will provide a long period of interest?

Where to plant your trees

The positioning of trees in a garden depends on their purpose. In small city and suburban gardens, you may want pleached trees (see pp.82–83) or a small copse to provide privacy or disguise an ugly view. You can use either a group of standard trees or multi-stems – do not mix them – and use a single species to create more impact.

You can also create a focal point with a specimen tree (see above centre). Consider where you will view this tree from: the lounge, an upstairs bedroom or the patio? If there is a spot in the garden where you can view the tree from all three areas, this will be the ideal location. A feature tree can also be used to disguise an ugly building or mask a view.

To create shade for a seating area, look at how the sun travels around your garden and position the tree where it casts a shadow at the times when you are going to be sitting there. I mentioned umbrella trees earlier in this book (see above right, and p.83) which can also be used to shade a patio. Perfect for small gardens, they do not take up much space and will not block the neighbour's natural light.

Espalier fruit trees (see above left) are suitable for both large and small gardens, and should be planted about 60cm/24in away from a wall or fence, or next to a free-standing framework.

DECIDUOUS TREES FOR SMALL GARDENS

Amelanchier lamarckii
White flowers in spring; berries and fiery red leaves in autumn.

***Cersis canadensis* 'Avondale'**
Covered in deep pink pea like flowers in spring.

***Magnolia × soulangeana* 'Satisfaction'** Has a compact bushy habit.

***Cornus kousa* 'White Fountain'**
Masses of white flowers in spring; brick red, pinks and golds in autumn.

***Prunus* 'Little Pink Perfection'**
Abundance of pinkish red buds, which open in clusters.

***Euonymus europaeus* 'Red Cascade'** Blazing scarlet foliage and orange-pink, winged fruit in autumn.

EVERGREEN TREES FOR SMALL GARDENS

Eriobotrya japonica
Distinct heavily veined foliage; ideal for small gardens.

Arbutus unedo
Small bell-shaped flowers that produce a honey fragrance.

Olea europaea
Small silver-grey leaves and drought tolerant

***Juniperus scopulorum* 'Blue Arrow'** Aromatic steely-blue foliage; perfect for formal, Italianate-style gardens.

***Eucalyptus gunnii* FRANCE BLEU ('Rengun')** Silvery blue foliage and the classic aroma of Eucalyptus.

Chamaerops humilis
 Fan-shaped leaves and slow growing; perfect for an exotic-style garden or balcony.

How do I choose low-maintenance planting?

Just as your home needs maintenance, so will your garden. However, by choosing suitable plants you can avoid an endless 'to do' list.

By reducing the number of different plants in your palette and repeating a chosen few in the design, you can limit the seasonal maintenance. Choose plants that need maintaining at the same time of the season. Also choose plants that are slow growing, which will reduce the need for frequent pruning or cutting back.

A low maintenance garden can be created with evergreen shrubs such as pittosporums, *Osmanthus*,

Viburnum tinus, *Choisya* and hebes. The focus is then on shapes, shades of green, foliage and texture. Lower-growing sub-shrubs that also have woody stems can be incorporated into the mix, too. Note that sub-shrubs are low growing woody perennials, they are not evergreen. However, low maintenance gardens do not have to lack flowers and colour. Small trees such as *Amelanchier lamarckii*, *Malus sargentii* 'Tina' and *Euonymus europaeus* 'Red Cascade' offer flowers and colourful fruits and need little or no pruning. The evergreen star jasmine (*Trachelospermum jasminoides*) has small, white, scented flowers and does not require much maintenance, apart from tying some of its stems to a framework or wires. *Hydrangea anomola* subsp. *petiolaris* is another easy climber – it clings to walls and fences unaided, so does not need training. Plant these against untreated walls that will not need painting.

Some ornamental grasses such as *Stipa gigantea*, *Pennisetum alopecuroides* 'Hameln', *Anemanthele lessoniana* and *Hakonechloa macra* provide long periods of interest and are easy to look after.

For additional floral colour, try *Baptisia australis*, *Erysimum* 'Bowles's Mauve', *Geranium psilostemon*, *Salvia* 'Royal Bumble', *Phlomis russeliana*, *Cistus* 'Silver Pink', *Stachys byzantina* and *Nepeta* 'Walkers Low'.

Make sure your planting borders are full and mulched to help prevent weeds and reduce water evaporation rates.

Planning your *planting*

~~~~~~

The next step is to create a planting plan for your garden (see p.52).

Once you have positioned your trees and structural shrubs on your plan, you can start having fun layering the perennials, grasses, shrub roses and ferns. Don't forget to dress your fences with climbers, too. Position taller plants at the back of the border and shorter ones towards the front, threading a few bigger plants with see-through stems such as *Stipa gigantea* dotted through the border here and there. Plants with tall flower spikes such as *Verbascum* or *Eremurus* can also be used in this way. Working them back and forth through your borders will create movement and rhythm.

Our brains are designed to appreciate groupings in odd numbers. To create impact in borders, garden designers place plants in groups of three, five, seven, and so forth. Only specimen plants such as trees and shrubs are planted singly. Use this trick in your planting scheme, and remember to repeat some varieties of plants through all the borders. This will unite the planting and take the eye from one area to the next. Another trick is to plant grasses such as *Nassella tenuissima* as foils for colourful plants like geums and penstemons, making them stand out. This grass will also repeat the soft texture and movement of other species, such as *Stipa gigantea*.

How do I create planting layers?

Having looked at the hierarchy of plants in a forest (see p.140), apply those principles to your garden to create three planting layers. The upper layer consists of trees and tall shrubs that are at eye level or above. The next is made up of shrubs and sub-shrubs that create a visual mass, and below those are the fillers, which comprise perennials, ferns, grasses and ground cover. Each layer is connected to the next and by staggering the plants you will create a flow and depth to your planting. It is through scale, proportion, repetition, flow, and depth that designers create the gardens you see in the magazines.

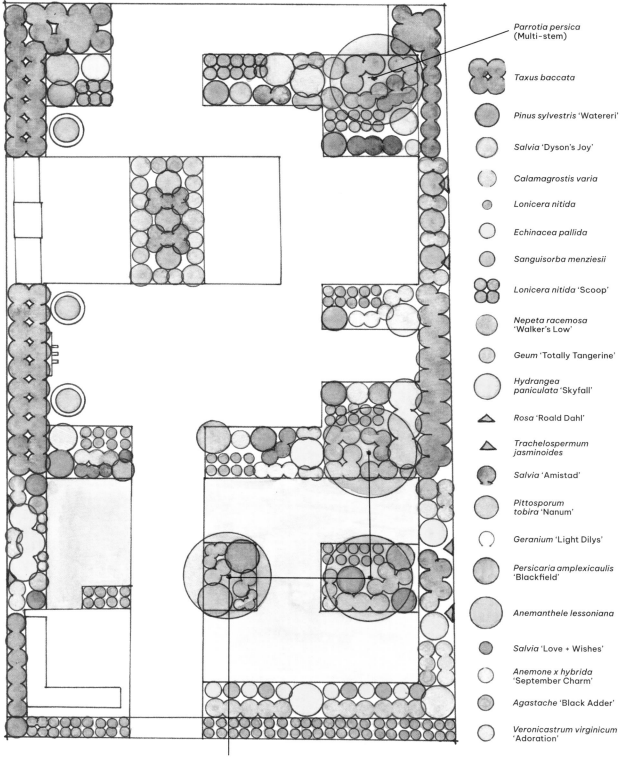

Parrotia persica
(Multi-stem)

Taxus baccata

Pinus sylvestris 'Watereri'

Salvia 'Dyson's Joy'

Calamagrostis varia

Lonicera nitida

Echinacea pallida

Sanguisorba menziesii

Lonicera nitida 'Scoop'

Nepeta racemosa 'Walker's Low'

Geum 'Totally Tangerine'

Hydrangea paniculata 'Skyfall'

Rosa 'Roald Dahl'

Trachelospermum jasminoides

Salvia 'Amistad'

Pittosporum tobira 'Nanum'

Geranium 'Light Dilys'

Persicaria amplexicaulis 'Blackfield'

Anemanthele lessoniana

Salvia 'Love + Wishes'

Anemone x hybrida 'September Charm'

Agastache 'Black Adder'

Veronicastrum virginicum 'Adoration'

Amelanchier lamarckii (Multi-stem)

Repetition in planting

As well as looking at layers in terms of plant height, think about the repetition and rhythm in your scheme. By repeating the same forms, shapes, colours, or textures you create a visual pacing that leads the eye around the garden. You can repeat the same plants or use different types that share the same shape or leaf form. Garden designers often use spherical or cushion shapes in the form of clipped *Ilex crenata*, *Pittosporum* or yew (*Taxus baccata*). These can be different sizes, but the same shape. The undulation of these forms also adds to the rhythm within the borders.

Repetition and rhythm are not just limited to shrubs. Grasses, ferns, herbaceous perennials and bulbs will work in the same way. Following this planting method will not only unify your borders but also help to minimize their maintenance.

Plant precautions
If you have very young children or pets, check that your plant selections are not poisonous. Better to be safe than sorry. Some plants such as euphorbias can cause skin irritation, so wear gloves when handling them.

Planting for the whole year

When designing a garden, a common mistake is using plants that only perform in spring and summer, when your outdoor space is there to be enjoyed through all the seasons, including winter. Evergreen trees and shrubs will provide year-round interest, as will deciduous trees that offer a beautiful branch structure or colourful bark. Trees that grow as natural columns such as *needle pine* (*Cupressus sempervirens* 'Pyramidalis') or fastigiate yew (*Taxus fastigiata*) are good choices for small spaces, or consider shrubs that have been topiarized, such as a multi-stemmed *Osmanthus burkwoodii* with a mushroom head or an *Ilex crenata* shaped into an onion dome.

Include flowers that bloom in winter and early spring, too. For instance, *Clematis cirrhosa* 'Jingle Bells' flowers from early winter to late winter, while witch hazels (*Hamamelis*) come into flower in January and emit the most divine scent. *Edgeworthia* flowers in late winter and also offers a wonderful scent. Then there are the early-flowering bulbs such as crocus, snowdrops and some narcissi. Before making your final choices, check that your garden offers the conditions your plants prefer; which months of the year will they be in leaf and flower; and their ultimate heights and spreads. This information will help you to design a scheme that will provide interest throughout the seasons using plants that will thrive in your site.

Even the best garden designers and horticulturalists suffer some plant failures, so don't be discouraged if you lose a few. Keep a diary of failures and successes and compile a monthly log of your plants' seasonal performances. You could even take photos and stick them into your gardening diary. These records will help you to make good purchases in the future as your garden develops.

For year round general garden maintenance, refer to the Monthly Garden Maintenance Diary on my website at: manojmaldegardendesign.co.uk/ monthly-garden-maintenance-diary

When should I plant bulbs?

Before planting bulbs, I let my other plants establish for a few seasons. I then look at where the gaps are in the borders and fill these spaces with bulbs that will add elements of surprise and colour when they bloom. There is a huge variety of bulbs, corms and tubers to choose from. The spring-flowering kind should be planted from early to late autumn. These include daffodils (*Narcissus*), tulips, alliums, *Camassia*, anemones, crocuses, *Eremurus*, *Cyclamen coum*, *Fritillaria*, *Ixia*, nerines and trilliums.

Those that flower in the summer are planted in spring. These include dahlias, cannas, lilies, *Crinum*, *Cardiocrinum*, *Chasmanthe* and *Eucomis*.

The foliage of some, for example alliums and *Camassia*, dies down and looks tatty as these plants start to bloom, so plant them behind later-flowering species that will disguise the withering leaves.

Bulbs in the green
If you are a snowdrop (*Galanthus*) fan, buy them in leaf, known as 'in the green', after they have finished flowering. Snowdrop bulbs can often dry out in transit, and planting them in leaf increases their chances of establishing successfully. Similarly, dog's tooth violet (*Erythronium*) are best bought as plants, as they hate drying out.

Planting
borders

Once you have assessed the sunny and shady spots in the garden as well as the soil type (see pp.42–43), you will understand which plants will thrive where. Regardless of aspect and conditions, prepare the soil well and mulch your borders to give your plants the best possible chance to establish. Here are some ideas for different sites and styles of border.

Hot sunny border

Start with the cornerstone elements: if you choose to put in trees, opt for those that have a delicate, open canopy that will let lots of light through to the underplanting. Many designers like using *Amelanchier lamarckii*. If you choose not to have trees, I would recommend some structural plants such as fastigiate yews or horneam (*Carpinus betulus*) clipped into columns to provide vertical interest, while *Ilex crenata* or yew balls or cushions will provide additional interest and structure.

For the back of the border, try *Inula helenium*, an impressive plant with yellow daisies on tall stems that will quickly fill a gap, and *Salvia* 'Pink Amistad', an elegant sage that has strong, upright stems and deep pink buds that open to soft pink blooms, loved by bees. It will also do well in pots.

Soften your planting scheme with grasses such *Stipa gigantea* or *Pennisetum alopecuroides* 'Hameln'. Weave these throughout the border. Other perennials to consider are *Sanguisorba officinalis* 'Red Thunder' or 'Pink Tanna'. These elegant plants produce slender stems topped with colourful lozenge-shaped flowers above ferny foliage. When the breeze catches them, they also add movement. If you are a fan of roses plant them in groups of at least three shrubs to create impact. *Rosa* 'Hot Chocolate' forms rusty orange buds which open to trusses of smoky-brown blooms that have a lovely scent.

I also love to use *Agastache* 'Black Adder' for the back or middle of a border, with its aromatic foliage and tiny, smoky, violet flowers on long stems resembling bottlebrushes. Other favourites include *Rudbeckia triloba*, with its yellow flowers and dark central cones on wiry stems; the flat, rusty-coloured flowerheads of *Achillea* 'Terracotta'; and *Salvia yangii* 'Blue Spire', with its aromatic foliage and upright spikes of violet-blue flowers.

Your next lower layer could include *Coreopsis verticillata* 'Moonbeam', which produces masses of buttery yellow daisy flowers on slender stems; *Penstemon* 'Pensham Plum', with its plum-purple flowers with white throats; and the frothy, wispy foliage and silver-green plumes of *Nasella tenuissima*. Other options are *Geum* 'Mai Tai', its pink-flushed apricot flowers rising above round, lobed foliage, and the scalloped leaves of *Alchemilla mollis*, which look beautiful when they catch droplets of rainwater. They also produce a froth of chartreuse flowerheads.

If you have a wall or fence, try climbing roses partnered with a clematis (both will need some form of support to climb up). By combining these you will extend the season of interest.

Support for climbers
When growing climbers that need support, create a framework to tie the stems on to. Install a trellis on a wall, or use horizontal 3–5mm/0.1–0.2in galvanized wires that you can feed through eyelets screwed into fence posts or bricks in walls. Finish off at the ends with a mechanism that will help you to tighten the wires so they are taught.

Dry shade border

Planting areas of dry shade, such as those under large, mature trees, can be challenging. However, this does not mean that no plants will survive there. For structure, try *Mahonia aquifolium*. Its glossy evergreen leaves provide year-round interest and clusters of yellow flowers appear in early spring when many plants are still dormant, followed by dark berries. Butcher's broom (*Ruscus aculeatus*), with its glossy green leaves and red berries, and the evergreen *Berberis* x *stenophylla* 'Corallina Compacta', which bears orange-yellow spring blooms, are other good choices for a middle layer.

The deciduous male fern *Dryopteris filix-mas* copes well in dry shade, its feathery fronds unfurling to form a distinctive shuttlecock shape. This fern turns a coppery tone in autumn. For something lighter to provide movement and structure on the edge of a tree canopy use *Anemanthele lessoniana*. Its slender, arching, evergreen foliage emerges green and then turns yellow, orange and red, while feathery sprays of airy flowerheads appear in summer.

For your lower layers, plant *Liriopi muscari* 'Big Blue'. It has evergreen, grass-like foliage and produces wands of violet flowers in autumn and dark berries in winter. *Bergenia* 'Abendglut' is another good choice for dry shade. Its large, oval, evergreen leaves turn a maroon colour in winter and magenta blooms rise above the foliage in spring.

Epimedium x *versilcolor* 'Sulphureum' is a beautiful evergreen perennial that makes good ground cover in dry, shady areas. Its buttery yellow blooms rise above the heart-shaped leaves, helping to bring light into darker spots. Another valuable ground-cover plant that copes extremely well with dry shade is *Euphorbia amygdaloides* var. *robbiae*. Long-lasting, lime green flowers rise above rosettes of glossy, dark green leaves and it works well in front of butcher's broom. At the front of the border, dot in a few *Cyclamen coum* for spring blooms and *C. hederifolium* for pink autumn flowers and a carpet of beautifully marbled, heart-shaped leaves.

Damp shade border

Damp shade with moisture retentive, humus-rich soil opens up a world of exciting planting possibilities. Think about the layers of plants that grow along a riverbank. You can create an upper canopy using river birch (*Betula nigra*), aptly named because it likes damp conditions. It is best known for its beautiful pink-brown bark that darkens as it ages and peels to reveal creamy-white tones underneath. It also has ovate green leaves with serrated edges that turn a glorious golden colour in autumn, and catkins offer interest in spring. *Carpinus betulus* (hornbeam) also copes with damp conditions, its bright green, heavily ribbed, serrated leaves providing an orangey golden show in autumn. It also produces catkins. Both trees look beautiful as multi-stemmed specimens.

For height at the back of the border, *Disporum longistylum* 'Green Giant' will form a tall, dense clump of upright stems, lush green leaves and yellowish-green bell-shaped flowers from late spring that then turn into glossy black fruit. Disporums are relatively rare and highly sought after by garden designers for their elegant form. *Eupatorium cannabinum* is a robust easy-to-grow plant for damp spots. Red-flushed stems with attractive lobed leaves are crowned in late summer with large flat-topped umbels of pink, purple or white flowers, loved by butterflies. The grass *Deschampsia cespitosa* will also tolerate partial shade and damp conditions and produces lovely soft clouds of silver-tinted, purple spikelets.

The salmon-red flowers of *Persicaria amplexicaulis* 'Firedance', loved by bees and butterflies, look stunning when this plant is grown en masse or try planting three clumps in different areas of a small garden. Further forward, add Japanese forest grass (*Hakonechloa macra*). This beautiful grass grows in a natural spherical shape. Dot single plants through the border or plant it in groups with drifts of *Astrantia major* var. *rosea* in between. Primulas look lovely growing along the water's edge and also cope well in part shade. Try *Primula vialii* for its crimson and lilac flower spikes or *Primula japonica* 'Miller's Crimson', with its upright stems of reddish-purple flowers. These make the most impact when grown in groups.

At the very front of the border plant *Hosta* 'Blue Mouse Ears', the leaves of which look like mouse ears; lilac flowers appear above them in summer. For a real wow factor, try planting drifts of *Tiarella* 'Pink Skyrocket' in damp, shady borders. This plant has deeply lobed green leaves with darker hues threading through them, while burgundy-flushed stems bearing clusters of tiny pink buds that open to reveal white star-shaped flowers appear in spring and early summer.

Tropical border

To create tropical borders, you need moist but well-drained, humus-rich soil. Also bear in mind that tropical plants can be high maintenance because many are tender and will need special protection or a heated greenhouse in winter.

Make deep borders that meet your pathways to create a rich jungle look, and mix foliage with bursts of flower colour. Build the upper story with large-leafed plants such as banana (*Musa basjoo*) with its green paddle-like leaves; *Ensete ventricosum* 'Maurelii', which also has large paddle-shaped foliage that is flushed with burgundy; *Fatsia japonica* to provide a hardy evergreen statement with its glossy palmate green leaves; and *Schefflera rhododendrifolia*, a reasonably hardy umbrella tree with deeply divided leaves on purple stems. Before investing in these plants, check their hardiness for your local climate and conditions as some may only be hardy to -10°C/14°F.

Others to consider include *Tetrapanax rex*, a hardy shrub bearing huge, deeply lobed, fresh green leaves, and hardy palms such as *Chamaerops humilis*, which is extremely tough and has fan-shaped green leaves that spread to create a very attractive form, and *Rhapidophyllum hystrix*, another fan-shaped hardy palm with glossy green leaves that have a dull silver underside. If you want a real show-stopping specimen, then the tender *Brahea armata* is worth spending your money on. This slow growing large palm has stunning silvery-blue fan-shaped leaves, but it will need winter protection. Multi-headed *Cordyline australis* are

hardy to -5°C/23°F and look like palms with their arching green sword-shaped leaves and grey corky bark.

The tree fern (*Dicksonia antarctica*), although not a tropical plant will certainly add to the jungle vibe, with its filigree-like fronds that unfurl into long leaves and chunky trunk formed of a mass of aerial roots. Tall ferns such as *Osmunda regalis* can be used in a middle layer, while the smaller *Cyrtomium fortunei* and tiny, dainty *Asplenium trichomanes* make good fillers below them.

Repeat the palmate foliage shapes of the *Fatsia* at a lower level with *Rodgersia pinnata* 'Superba' which will also produce clusters of pink flowers on tall stems above the purply-bronze leaves. *Echium pininana* will add a dramatic statuesque shape. This half-hardy biennial forms a leafy rosette in its first year, then a huge flower spike in the second year. It dies after flowering but produces thousands of seeds.

Add climbers such as *Trachelospermum jasminoides*, *Passiflora caerulea* or *Campsis* x *tagliabuana* 'Madame Galan' on walls and fences, and inject rich hot colours into your scheme with the striking striped leaves of *Canna* 'Durban', and the dahlias 'Chat Noir', 'La Recoleta', 'Perch Hill' and 'Nicholas'. The ginger lily (*Hedychium*) is also a must for a tropical border. Try *H.* 'Tara', *H. densiflorum* and *H. gardnerianum*. Other plants to include in your tropical borders are *Zantedeschia aethiopica*, *Lobelia tupa*, *Crocosmia* 'Hellfire' and *Tithonia rotundifolia*.

Mediterranean border

Mediterranean gardens are often created as gravel planting borders and require sunny positions and well-drained soil. The olive tree (*Olea europaea*), with its beautiful gnarled trunks and small sage-green leaves, and needle pines (*Cupressus sempervirens* 'Pyramidalis') lend a Mediterranean character. Hummocks of the lavender, *Lavandula angustifolia* 'Munstead', with its dense spikes of fragrant bluish-purple, flowers above silvery aromatic foliage; *Santolina rosmarinifolia* 'Lemon Fizz', which produces a compact mound of lime-green aromatic foliage and lemon-coloured button-like flowers, and the lilac-blue blooms of *Teucrium fruticans*, its silvery aromatic leaves clipped into loose balls or cushions, all provide structure for a Mediterranean-themed design. *Cistus* 'Silver Pink' is another good shrub choice.

Dress walls and fences in the salmon-red trumpet flowers of *Campsis* x *tagliabuana* 'Madame Galan', jasmine (*Jasminum officinalis*), or a climbing or rambling rose.

Guara (*Oenothera lindheimeri* 'Whirling Butterflies') will add both grace and frothiness to your borders, with its wispy stems of star-shaped white flowers that dance in the breeze. *Stipa gigantea* dotted among the hummocks of structural shrubs will add height and movement with its clumps of slender foliage and golden oat-like flowerheads, while *Salvia yangii* 'Blue Spire' planted in groups will add aromatic foliage and spikes of violet-blue flowers. The flowers of *Oenothera* and *Salvia* are both magnets for pollinators, too. *Stachys byzantina* 'Big Ears' will bring a velvety texture into your scheme with its soft silver-grey foliage and spikes of woolly pinkish-purple flowers. *Felicia amelloides* 'Felicitara Blue', a compact sub-shrub with masses of Wedgewood-blue daisy flowers, is a good choice for the edge of a pathway where it will soften the hardscaping. Also try combining *Nassella lessingiana* and alliums with their pompon flowers, and use multi-headed species tulips such as *Tulipa turkistanica* or *T. sylvestris* towards the front of the borders, followed by the California poppy (*Eschscholzia californica*) and *Erigeron karvinskianus*, both of which are prolific self-seeders.

Your Outdoor Room

Coastal border

Plants that thrive near the coast are tolerant of wind and salt spray, but planting windbreaks,such as hedges, will broaden your choices. *Griselinia littoralis*, with its ovate lime-coloured leaves, makes a fast-growing evergreen hedge; it can also be grown as a shrub or small tree. Another evergreen option is *Elaeagnus pungens* 'Maculata', a fast-growing salt- and wind-tolerant hedging plant with variegated leaves and tiny but extremely fragrant flowers. Also consider hornbeam (*Carpinus betulus*), which will often retain its golden autumn leaves into early winter. Phormiums can also create a shelter belt around your garden.

Multi-headed *Cordyline australis*, with arching sword-shaped leaves and grey corky bark, also fares well in the milder temperatures on the coast. *Pinus pinea*, often found around the Mediterranean coast, has greyish-green needles and cones with edible pine nuts. *Acacia dealbata* is a fast-growing evergreen tree with a spreading crown of fern-like leaves. Its bright yellow fragrant flowers look like small fluffy balls. *Crataegus persimilis* 'Prunifolia' is a deciduous tree that has a broad, rounded canopy and deep green leaves that turn orange and red in autumn; the white spring flowers are followed by red berries that attract birds.

Pittosporum tobira 'Nanum' is an attractive evergreen shrub with glossy green leaves and sweetly scented creamy-coloured flowers. It also grows successfully in containers and is great for balconies and roof gardens. These shrubs will provide beautiful structural hummock shapes with differing textures. Or opt for the dwarf pine (*Pinus mugo*), which produces a mound of dark green needles.

For shrubs with softer shapes, try *Caryopteris* x *clandonensis* 'Heavenly Blue', a densely branched deciduous shrub featuring green aromatic leaves with a silver underside and clusters of intense blue blooms that attract bees and butterflies. Evergreen *Bupleurum fruticosum* has glossy blue-green leaves and umbels of tiny yellow flowers. *Cistus creticus* produces masses of papery pink flowers with a yellow centre, and *Grevillea* 'Canberra Gem' has scented, green, needle-like leaves and pinky-red clusters of flowers. The silver-grey foliage of *Osmanthus rosmarinifolia* has tall stems of tiny flowers, attracting bees and butterflies. The red buds open to white in summer.

Add height and movement to a scheme using *Dierama pulcherrimum*. Bell-shaped, pale pink or magenta blooms dangle from delicate arching stems moving in the breeze.

For colour in your scheme use *Centranthus ruber*, *Erigeron glaucus* 'Sea Breeze', *Stachys byzantina*, *Pulsatilla vulgaris*, *Armeria maritima*, *Echium vulgare* and *Eryngium* x *zabelii* 'Big Blue'. Self-seeding poppies such as *Eschscholzia californica* and *Papaver rhoeas* are a must for any coastal garden, too.

Lawns

Should I include a lawn?

Lawns have been an obsession for the English for centuries. As lovely as they look, manicured lawns are high maintenance. They need feed and weed treatments in spring and autumn and copious amounts of water to keep them green during a dry summer, draining natural resources. You will also need a lawnmower and a place to store it. You may want to consider other options if you are time poor, but please try to avoid artificial lawns, which have a detrimental impact on the environment (see p.127), and consider other lawn alternatives instead (see pp.128–29).

How do I lay a lawn?

The best seasons to lay a lawn are early spring once the soil has warmed up or autumn, when the soil is still warm and seasonal rain will water the developing grass.

If you are intending to have a lawn, here are some tips on how to lay it.

- Test for drainage (see p.43).
- Assess the quality of your topsoil; a new lawn needs 10–15cm/4–6in of good quality, free-draining topsoil.
- Remove all weeds from the site.
- Prepare your soil for turfing by rotovating your soil when the soil is fairly dry.
- Rake over the soil so it resembles breadcrumbs, removing any stones.
- Remove large air gaps in the soil by walking over the site in boots, foot in front of foot, row by row.
- Purchase sterilized, weed-free topsoil from a reputable supplier if yours is poor quality. Lay it on top of the soil you have prepared and rake it out evenly over the surface. If you already have good quality topsoil, leave it for a couple of weeks and then remove any weeds that have grown. Give it the same preparation work as described above.
- Rake in a base 7:7:7 general purpose fertilizer that contains equal quantities of nitrogen, potassium and phosphorus.
- A couple of days before your turf is due to arrive, water your soil well.
- Ideally, lay a lawn on a cool cloudy day.

— Arrange your turf delivery on the same day you are going to lay it so that it doesn't dry out. If the corners of the turf curl, you will find it very difficult to get those corners flat again.

— Lay your turf in a stretcher bond pattern like brickwork so the sections knit together well.

— Once laid, keep the lawn well-watered to encourage good root growth.

— Do not walk on the newly laid lawn for at least six weeks while the roots establish.

— If seeding a lawn, the same principles apply for preparing the soil. Scatter the seed and gently rake it into the soil. Add some bird-proof netting to prevent birds eating the seed.

— If you are planning on laying wildflower turf, bear in mind these prefer impoverished soil. To lower the nutrient content, remove any existing turf and some of the topsoil.

— A clover lawn will grow in the same conditions and soil as normal grass turf.

Your lawn should be the last item to be installed after the rest of the garden has been completed. If you are making a new garden from scratch, an existing lawn could be ruined during the building process, so my advice would be to lay a new one. The last thing you want is your brand-new garden to be let down by an unsightly lawn.

What are the best times to plant?

Trees When trees become dormant from late autumn to mid-winter nurseries will sell bare-root trees, which come with the roots exposed. They also sell root-ball trees during this period. These are trees where the roots are surrounded by soil and wrapped in hessian. Plant them as soon as they arrive and stake large trees or those with a dense canopy and small root ball to help prevent wind rock. Trees that have been grown in containers are also available and can be planted all year round, unless the soil is frozen or waterlogged.

Shrubs Most shrubs are available in containers throughout the year. However, some nurseries sell larger shrubs as root-ball specimens. The best time of the year to plant hardy shrubs is in autumn; those that are less hardy can be planted in spring.

Hedges Root-balled and bare-root hedging plants are available from late autumn to mid-winter, which is also the best time to plant them.

Roses Bare-root roses are available from mid-autumn to mid-winter, and can be a little cheaper than container-grown plants. Plant them as soon as you receive them. Container-grown roses can be planted at any time of the year, although spring and autumn are the best times.

Grasses, ferns and perennials These come as container-grown plants and are best planted in autumn or spring when some may become more readily available. These plants can be planted through summer, too, but they may suffer heat stress and will require more water to get them settled in.

Bulbs, corms and tubers Spring-flowering bulbs such as daffodils, tulips, alliums, anemones and *Camassia* should be planted in autumn. Plant tulips in late autumn to lessen the risk of a fungal disease called tulip fire affecting them. Snowdrops and bluebells are best planted in the green in early spring. Summer-flowering plants such as dahlias and cannas are planted in spring. Nurseries only sell bulbs, corms and tubers close to the planting time.

What depths of soil do I need?

The soil or compost depth in a pot will depend on the plants. As a basic guide:

- **Trees:** 90–120cm/3–4ft
- **Shrubs:** 60–90cm/24–36in
- **Grasses, ferns, perennials:** 40–50cm/16–20in
- **Annuals and bedding:** 15–30cm/6–12in
- **Alpines:** 10cm/4in

For bulbs, corms and tubers, the soil depth varies, depending on the size. As a guide they should be buried at least three to four times their depth, with a layer of soil underneath too.

How do I use *pots* in my garden?

Containers and pots add sculptural shapes, architecture and colour to a garden. They can make a big impact, especially when set against a solid colour such as a painted backdrop, but avoid using lots of small pots which can make the space look cluttered. Instead, choose three decent-sized pots, either set out in a group or placed individually along a path to create repetition. However, large pots can be expensive and heavy, so alternatively use just one as a focal point if money is tight or you have a small garden. And remember that not all pots have to be planted.

There are a whole host of pot materials to choose from, including metal, plastic, terracotta, ceramic, terrazzo, concrete, fibreglass and resin. Select those that suit the theme of your garden and make sure there are drainage holes at the bottom – you do not want the soil or compost to become waterlogged. Add crocks or stone chippings to the bottom of the pot to improve drainage – use broken pieces of polystyrene to reduce the weight on a balcony or roof terrace – and raise them up on feet to allow excess water to escape. This will also help reduce the risk of frost damage.

You could recycle old oil drums for containers for a rustic theme. Cut the tops off and clean them out thoroughly before making some drainage holes in the base. Then waterproof them inside with a coating of butyl paint. You could paint the outside in either a plain colour or be creative and decorate them with a scene or pattern to go with your theme. Old chimney pots imaginatively placed in borders will suit a country-cottage style. Plant them with spring bulbs followed by summer bedding such as fuchsias and pelargoniums, changing the displays as the seasons turn.

Plants in containers will dry out more easily than plants in the ground. To keep yours hydrated, you could install a micro-irrigation system with drippers, attached to a digital timer on the tap. Another option is to use a subterranean water tank in the container. This will need to be topped up occasionally. Adding water-retentive granules to the soil may also help. These release moisture as and when the plants need water. You could, of course, use drought-tolerant plants that require less water but this does not mean no water at all. Also add a slow-release fertilizer to the compost when the nutrients in it run out, usually after six to eight weeks. For permanent plants in pots, add fertilizer once a year in spring. Mulch the surface of the soil with small pebbles, gravel, or decorative glass aggregates to help reduce water evaporation.

How do I create a *container garden?*

If you are creating a container garden on a patio, balcony or roof terrace, just like your garden, you will need to check the size and shape of the space, the location of the doors and windows, the type of boundary, aspect and the views (see p.38 for site survey). In particular, note the dimensions of your access points – you don't want to buy a very large, heavy container that you are unable to get through the door.

Rather than doing a full site analysis you can add notes to your site survey. You can then develop your site survey into a concept plan and then a master plan. Finally, decide what size of containers can be positioned where and how much space you have for seating, as well as which walls would be best for vertical planting or a piece of artwork.

Choose a theme for your container garden, and link your indoor and outdoor spaces through colours or by bringing the styling of your interiors outside.

The wind and sun on balconies and roof gardens will quickly dry out containerized plants so choose drought-tolerant species and those that can tolerate the heat. Plants with waxy foliage such as *Pittosporum tobira* 'Nanam' or those with smaller leaves like *Euonymus japonicus* 'Green Spire' will cope well. Needle-like leaves such as those of *Pinus mugo* or rosemary (*Salvia rosmarinus*) are also good choices. Silver-leafed plants, including *Lavandula angustifolia* 'Hidcote', reflect light thereby reducing water loss through the foliage, while the hairs on the leaves of plants such as *Stachys byzantina* trap water as it evaporates thereby retaining humidity around them. Ornamental grasses such as *Calamagrostis brachytricha*, *Calamagrostis varia*, *Nassella tenuissima* and *Pennisetum alopecuroides* 'Hameln' will add texture and movement to the mix.

The olive tree (*Olea europaea*) copes well with wind and heat and it can be pruned to keep it smaller in a pot. Other options for structure include *Carpinus japonica* and *Osmanthus burkwoodii*. Floral colour can be introduced through *Oenothera lindheimeri*, *Felicia amelloides* 'Felicitara Blue', *Salvia nemorosa* 'Caradonna', *Nepeta* 'Walkers Low', *Achillea millefolium*, *Geranium wallichianum* 'Crystal Lake', *Cistus* x *purpureus* and *Erigeron karvinskianus*. Also try one of my favourites which is *Verbena officinalis* var. *grandiflora* 'Bampton'. This has slender bronze stems topped with spikes of small violet-pink flowers and creates a light airy clump. Climbers such as the evergreen *Trachelospermum jasminoides* with its scented flowers could cover the walls, while bulbs will offer a spring surprise when they pop up.

Just because you are limited to a small outdoor space does not mean you cannot grow some of your own produce. Living walls are ideal for cut-and-come-again lettuces, bush cherry tomatoes, chard and other edibles. Or grow produce alongside your ornamentals in containers. Try peas, chillies, aubergines, spring onions, vine tomatoes and other varieties you like to eat. Nasturtiums not only look pretty but both the leaves and edible flowers have a peppery taste and make a lovely addition to salads. Pot marigold (*Calendula*) is also very pretty. The peppery petals can be added to ice cubes, adding some colour to a gin and tonic, or you can include them in omelettes.

Weight-loading for balconies and roof gardens

The weight of wet soil, pots and plants on balconies and roof gardens needs to be considered to ensure they do not exceed the load-bearing capacity. If using lots of pots and you are not sure what this capacity is, call in a structural engineer to check that your garden will be safe. To lighten the load, you can use special soil designed for roof terraces and avoid heavy materials such as stone. Also think about drainage; neighbours will not be happy if water leaks into their space, so again use a professional to ensure this will not be an issue.

6

Pulling it all together

You have designed your garden. So far it is just a vision on paper but now begins the exciting task of making your design a reality. Just like an extension of your home, treat your garden as you would an interior room when taking the final step in the design process. Once a room in your home is painted or wallpapered, attention turns to the finer details such as curtains, furniture, soft furnishings and artworks for the walls. Apply this same principle to your garden.

To pull your design together and turn it into a beautiful, functional area, choose items to dress the space. The first thing you will want is furniture. Perhaps some stunning containers on your patio to tie this area to the rest of the garden? How about a piece of sculpture as a focal point? Or some lamps or fairy lights? Take your time choosing these details. Not everything needs to be done in one go. The fun part of this stage is sourcing exactly the right pieces.

Bringing your *design* to *life*

Now you have designed your garden you are ready to start on the build, but before you begin, take time to look at your plan and break down the building processes. Note each step on paper or your computer and, like a good landscape contractor, create a step-by-step schedule. This is the order in which the garden will be constructed. And remember to laminate your plans to protect them when you take them outside.

Keeping control of the budget

As well as creating a schedule of works, put together a spreadsheet to assess the costs. Insert columns for item, quantity, unit cost, total cost, supplier and delivery dates, and then fill the chart with all the items and materials you will need to build your garden. This is a good way to assess the total costs and make savings, if needed. For example, you may find the basalt slabs you wanted for your patio are too expensive but sandstone or porcelain are more affordable options, or you could create a border using setts, thereby reducing the number of slabs needed, or reduce the size of the patio.

Focus on the hierarchy of expenditure, prioritizing the bones of the garden such as the hard landscaping and structural plants. These are expensive items to change every few years, therefore spending money on quality products and plants will help your garden stand the test of time.

If you have a small garden, you may only need limited quantities of some materials so look at end-of-stock lines. You might also find that professional contractors have materials left over from a job that they need to sell on, so look for these on the marketplace pages of social media platforms or freecycle sites. Also phase the work to allow you time to save for the garden you want.

OTHER COST SAVING TIPS

— Seed a lawn rather than turfing it.
Yes, it takes longer to establish, but
it will save you money.
— Buy young trees and let them
establish over time.
— Buy trees and hedging plants in
autumn and winter during the bare
root or root-balled season.
— Some nurseries sell perennials in
small pot sizes for less than larger
plants. If you plant these at the right
time they will establish very quickly.
— An alternative is to buy perennials
in a large pot. If you are skilled
at dividing plants, you can then
split each plant into three and
immediately increase your stock.
— Join a gardening club. The gardening
community is incredibly generous and
will swap plants and share advice.
— Look on the freecycle pages.
Recycling is important and stops
waste from going into landfill.
— Source your materials through
builders' merchants or specialist
suppliers that sell to the public.
They will have good knowledge of
the products they stock and will be
competitively priced.
— Buy your plants from nurseries or
reputable garden centres. Their
knowledgeable staff can offer advice
and they stock healthy, quality
plants. You will also be supporting
some of the smaller local businesses.

How do I implement my design?

The first job when installing a garden is to get rid of what you don't need. Carefully dig up any plants that you plan to keep but want to reposition and pot them up.

Throughout the build, it is important to keep your site clean, tidy and safe, and remember to wear protective clothing such as steel-capped boots and protective gloves while you are working. The general process will be as follows, but do bear in mind this could change, depending on your design:

— Before work starts, take photos of boundaries in case any disputes arise during the construction of your garden.

— Implement any protection that is required to neighbouring properties, such as Heras fencing (this can be hired). Cover this with debris netting.
— Start clearing the site. This should include any unwanted vegetation and lawn and all problematic weeds such as mares' tail.
— If you have Japanese knotweed, this needs to be cleared by specialist companies.
— Have a designated storage area for your tools.
— Attend to boundary lines. Any damaged fence panels must be replaced. If all fencing is to be replaced, this should be done now. Be aware of any boundary disputes.
— Once the site is cleared, mark out your design lines on the ground using a marker spray. Referring to your setting out plan, mark the patio or deck, pathways, steps, walls, planting borders, other social areas, structures and water features. Check your measurements regularly.
— Put in stakes and string lines. Check levels of string lines with a spirit level and tape measure (see p.41).
— Excavate areas, move soil, grade soil to create a slope, or build up levels.
— Deal with any known drainage issues.
— Dig tree pits and plant trees.
— Carry out the first fix for electrics. Engage a qualified electrician to lay cabling for lighting.
— If irrigation is to be installed, lay any hidden pipework required.
— Install sub-base/foundations for patio, pathways, level changes, steps, and any walling or raised beds.

- Paint boundary fences if this is a required part of the design.
- Lay patio slabs. Keep checking levels, making sure the fall is in the right direction and at the correct fall rate.
- Construct retaining walls, steps, raised patios or decks.
- Remember to allow for light fittings in hardscape areas – discuss this with your electrician.
- Install pathway edging and lay pathway material.
- Once your hardscape areas are installed, lay some protection over them to avoid any damage.
- Install structures such as pergolas, sheds, arbours, arches or screens.
- Install edging to planting borders if part of the design.
- Prepare the soil in your planting borders by adding organic matter. Mix it into the soil by digging it through or laying it as a mulch (see p.43).
- Finish laying irrigation.
- Install light fittings in the borders (second fix). This must be carried out by a qualified electrician.
- Plant new shrubs.
- Plant climbers, ferns, roses, ornamental grasses and perennials. (You may wish to do this as part of a later phase to help with cash flow).
- Finish your borders with mulch at a depth of 5cm/2in minimum.
- If a lawn is included, prepare the soil, sow the seed or lay turf.
- Clean all hard surfaces and tidy the garden.
- Position your containers.
- Place your furniture and enjoy!

Foundations

If you plan to lay foundations yourself, there are some very good websites that show you how to create them for patios and pathways, or to build the supporting framework for a deck.

If these foundations are not constructed correctly, they can be dangerous and costly to repair, so employ a professional if you are not experienced and confident in hardscape construction. Remember these are the bones of your garden and an investment in your home.

What sort of *furniture* and *accessories* do I need?

Stay true to the theme of your garden by sourcing furniture that suits the look, and do not clutter up the space or it may end up looking like a doctor's waiting room. Buy furniture that is in proportion with your garden size. If it's too big, it will dominate your space and make it feel smaller. Likewise, if it's too small, the furniture will look lost and make the area less of a destination.

If you have a small garden, consider buying either a dining table and chairs or a comfy sofa that you can lounge on, rather than both. If you choose a sofa, then you will need to eat off your lap. Buy what you will make most use of. Also keep furniture lightweight or choose chairs with some transparency that allow light through. In a small garden heavy furniture can look cumbersome and make the space feel enclosed.

You could also consider built-in cantilevered seating and use the space underneath for shade-loving plants. Extending the borders in this way also creates a feeling of space. You will need storage for cushions and other items, too – I often use benches with storage units underneath the seats to save space. When buying furniture, you can often get some great bargains if you wait until the end of the season sales.

There are many lovely accessories on the market to dress your garden. As with furniture, be selective and avoid cluttering it with too many items. For a small garden think about accessories with a dual purpose. For example, a storage box could be perfect for your sofa cushions but also act as a seat, while a decorative parasol will also provide shade. Or choose lanterns that look beautiful by day and bring a cosy glow to your patio in the evening. How about garden accessories that will invite wildlife such as a bird bath, a bird box, or a beehive? A beautifully designed firepit that will take off the chill on a cool evening. Soft furnishings such as throw cushions, outdoor rugs and blankets will also help to add colour and comfort.

Choosing garden furniture materials

Rattan Many pieces are synthetic imitations of natural rattan, so pay attention to what you're buying. Often used in wicker furniture as well, rattan is a vinelike plant that is tough, durable, and reasonably weatherproof. It is light enough to move around the garden and available as outdoor sofas, loungers and dining sets. Rattan furniture will suit most traditional styles of gardens. Synthetic rattan furniture can be left outside in winter but do put away any cushions. It is advisable to move natural rattan furniture indoors or put waterproof covers over them.

Metal Choose from traditional wrought iron vintage furniture or classical styles to suit an English country cottage look, or opt for modern metal pieces for a contemporary garden. Wrought iron is tough, durable and can be painted in different colours, but if left outside all year, it can be prone to rust. The frames of contemporary sofas, benches, and bistro and dining sets are often made from powder-coated steel or aluminium, although these materials can also blend into a rural or cottage-style garden. They are also lighter in weight than wrought iron, easier to move around and low maintenance.

Wood A wonderful material for both modern and classical styles of furniture, wood suits many garden designs. Consider furniture that shows off the wood's natural form and characteristics, and look out for blocks of green oak if you want simple stools. If you are good at carpentry, you may even want to make some of your own furniture. It is advisable to cover wooden furniture in winter, and oil it annually in autumn before you put it away. Remember that all wood fades to a silver tone, so it will need staining, oiling or painting to maintain a vibrant look. Also check that the furniture you buy has an FSC label, showing the timber is from a sustainable source.

Plastic Strong, durable and lightweight, plastic can be moulded into different designs and is available in every colour. Plastic furniture is more suited to contemporary garden styles, and it is easy to maintain, often stackable and can be a cost-effective option. Keep an eye out for recycled plastic furniture and check that any plastics you do buy can be recycled.

Concrete Suitable for a modern style of garden, concrete is not as popular as other materials, partly due to its weight and limited colour palette. Furniture is made from either fibre or moulded cement and you can buy stools, tables and chairs, though the colour options are limited to a couple of shades of grey. However, do keep in mind that concrete does have a high carbon footprint.

Stone Used in various styles from contemporary, English country cottage to Mediterranean, in their natural state, flat-faced stones can act as both sculptural forms as well as a cooling place to perch. Stone boulders are heavy to move, so make sure you put them in the right position. You really don't want to move them more than necessary.

How do I *style* my garden?

When styling your garden, think of materials, paint colours, ornaments and furnishings that will enhance your chosen theme. You may find it easier to refer to your mood board again at this stage, or create a new one with images of furniture and accessories you like. This may help you to check that the final styling works with your theme. As a jumping-off point, here are three examples of how styling fits different themes.

Contemporary style

For a contemporary garden, think modern materials and clean, crisp shapes and lines. Powder-coated aluminium furniture, available in some beautiful colours, or wood and chrome combinations would all work well. Look out for stools, chairs and tables in fibre cement, or furniture made from moulded plastic to provide a flash of colour in the garden. Dress your furniture with simple blocks of colour through soft furnishings or opt for geometrics prints.

For containers, look at simple, clean shapes. GRP (glass-fibre reinforced plastic) and powder-coated aluminium containers will suit your theme. If you are using concrete for the hard landscaping, weathered steel planters will add to the modern look. Also try contemporary pieces of glass or ceramics on your dining or coffee table.

Country cottage style

This style is all about the romance of yesteryear: pretty colours, beautiful florals and shabby chic, vintage or retro detailing. How about a wooden tabletop with old Singer sewing machine legs and mismatched wooden chairs? You could dress your furniture with retro print cushions, use an oil cloth to cover the dining table and decorate your space with vintage ceramics. Have some fun with lighting by using fairy light or recycling jam jars with tea lights (see p.100). Create your containers from old tin buckets or half whisky barrels – the latter can also be made into small aquatic gardens. Just make sure you drill some drainage holes in the bottom of any plant containers. You could then include some old tinplate signage on the walls, add bunting around the frame of the pergola and use a vintage tiered cake stand to hold a few small potted plants.

Moroccan style

Moroccan gardens are all about rich colours and geometric patterns. Greens, yellows, and cobalt are perfect for the theme, teamed with the earthy tones of oranges, clay pinks and sandy taupe, plus gold or copper.

When choosing furniture, consider Moroccan leather poufs, mosaic-tiled tables, and cushions created from old kilim textiles. You may even want to throw down a kilim rug. Wall screens decorated with the eight-pointed star geometrical pattern will add to the mood, especially when backlit. Add to the theme with wooden benches and side tables with bone inlay and some stunning Moroccan lanterns. Many of these items will need to be brought inside over winter, so check you have adequate storage space. Choose terracotta or ceramic containers and use Moroccan pottery to dress your table. A water feature finished with printed tiles inspired by the Moorish mosaic patterns from the Alhambra will complete the look.

How do I use *focal points* in the garden?

〜〜〜〜〜〜〜〜〜〜〜〜〜〜〜〜〜〜〜〜〜〜〜〜〜

Whilst you will have considered the focal points at the beginning of the design process, implementing them will help to bring the whole garden together. Apart from drawing the eye and helping to define a journey, there are various other reasons why designers use focal points in the garden. They can aid in creating cohesion between the home and the garden. Focal points can also create drama and theatre in a space, or even stir up emotions, becoming a point of conversation or part of a sensory experience. You can use them as elements of surprise as you journey through the garden; create calm spaces where the eye can rest before moving on or to divert attention away from an ugly view.

What can I use as focal points?

There are no hard or fast rules about what makes a focal point – just make sure yours respond to your theme. A piece of sculpture by an artist whose work you really like could work well – if it is small, simply raise it on a podium. Although you may want to consider the position of a piece of sculpture at the design stage, the choice can be made once the garden is complete. Sometimes you must live with a piece of art and see if it suits the space, checking how it looks during the day and at night.

A specimen tree with stunning branch structure and bark interest, or a beautiful water feature can also be a focal point. In Islamic gardens, a central water feature acts as a sensory focal point with a practical purpose, as it helps to cool the air during the heat of the day. In a contemporary garden use pots to give vibrant bursts of colour, or paint an old timber bench a bright shade and place it so that your eye gravitates towards it. I also love the idea of an onion-shaped love seat surrounded by ornamental grasses to attract attention.

A timber arbour with fairy lights coiled around it can become a focal point at night. Or, if you have a view of a spectacular feature, such as a church steeple, why not frame that and turn it into a focal point?

In a Mediterranean-style garden, you could use a pithoi or large stone container among the planting. Alternatively, turn the container into a brimming water feature or simply lay it on its side to draw the eye.

Where do I place focal points?

When designing a garden, it is worth looking at where your focal points are going to be at the start of the design process, so that they are integral to the whole scheme and do not look like an afterthought.

The idea of focal points is to draw attention to a particular area and they can also create a reason for the viewer to journey to that destination and stop. Garden designers often use the lines of the property as axes to find these sweet spots for focal points. For example, if you want one that can be viewed from a few different positions both indoors and outdoors, check the lines of sight as you look out of the windows and doors to decide where to place it.

Some popular places for focal points include:

— At the end of a garden pathway.
— Where two lines cross, as in Islamic gardens where this point is marked with a central water feature.
— Where a pathway changes direction.
— Where the garden changes levels to a more open space
— A sculpture in a pond. This can be on a pedestal to make it look as if it's floating on the water, and you will see the reflection on the surface.
— Sculptures in a meadow or prairie planting, which can look amazing, especially when lit by low winter sun.
— Beautiful laser-cut panels on a dull wall or fence – they will look even better if backlit.
— Striking pots either in planting borders or placed symmetrically along a pathway, as often seen in Italianate gardens.
— A fireplace, possibly set into a wall to one side of a patio.
— A well-designed firepit that can be both practical and a piece of sculpture.

Aftercare

∿∿∿∿∿∿∿∿∿∿∿∿∿∿∿∿∿∿∿∿∿∿∿∿

Once you have turned your back yard into a beautiful garden, don't stop there. After all your creativity, hard work and investment, you want to make sure your outdoor space continues to look its best all year round. Maintain your garden like you would the rooms in your home. Little and often makes it seem less of a chore and will result in a space that you are proud of. Pick a handful of weeds every time you go out in the garden.

Is there really a 'no-maintenance' garden?

When designing your garden, try and keep in mind the amount of time you can commit to maintaining it. You do not want it to become a burden. While there is no such thing as a no-maintenance garden, you can reduce your garden maintenance time by avoiding overly manicured features such as striped lawns and opting for simple planted borders that look after themselves for much of the year. Leaving perennial plants to stand uncut over winter and not clearing up too many leaves lessens the load, and is also helpful to wildlife.

How do I maintain my hardscape areas?

All landscaping materials will need some upkeep but some are easier to maintain than others. Timber decking will need to be washed annually, either with a jet washer or hard bristle brush and soapy water. Once dry, you will also need to oil it (see p.71), although composite decking part produced with recycled materials may not need this treatment.

Sandstone is cheaper than limestone or Yorkstone, but it is a softer, more porous stone and prone to moss and algae growth, especially if used in a shady area. If not cleaned regularly it will become slippery and a trip hazard, so if you can afford limestone or Yorkstone, you will reduce the time needed for maintenance. However, all natural stone products

will need power washing occasionally to keep them clean and safe. Porcelain requires slightly less attention than natural stone, but even this will require some cleaning, as dirt inevitably builds up in all outdoor areas. In addition to washing, you will need to sweep off debris from your patio from time to time as well.

Apply the same maintenance regime to steps. If you cannot stretch to Yorkstone or limestone in a shaded area, consider gravel infill steps.

Young children enjoy being included in household chores and maintaining your outdoor space – pulling weeds, gathering sticks, raking leaves – can all be a game that gets them involved in the garden.

How do I maintain my lawn?

It is a common misconception that a low maintenance garden is one where most of it is laid to lawn. Lawns are not low maintenance, anything but. To have a perfect sward, a lawn needs to be scarified in autumn to remove moss and thatch and encourage healthy grass growth. The soil will also need to be aerated regularly to ensure oxygen reaches the roots and to prevent lawn compaction, which is the main cause of moss growth. Aeration can be carried out in spring or autumn by pushing a garden fork into the lawn to a depth of 15cm/6in at regular intervals, or using a lawn aerator, so the whole surface is covered in holes. It is best to apply some fertilizer immediately after aerating your lawn, too. Treat your lawn with a spring weed and feed, and repeat in autumn with a product designed for this time of year. Do make sure that you use the correct weed and feed for the season.

Lawns also need mowing. In spring, set your mower on its highest setting for the first cut and then lower the blades as the weeks pass. As a general rule of thumb, a fortnightly cut should be sufficient, or once a week in summer. However, the frequency depends on how quickly your grass is growing. Do not set the lawn mower so low that it ends up scalping it; leaving the grass a little longer allows it to photosynthesize efficiently and produce more food for itself. If there is a drought, do not mow the lawn or water established lawns. Grass is very resilient and will green up as soon as rain returns – I've had a completely brown lawn in summer that was green again within four days of rain.

If you have wildflowers growing through your grass, you may not want to mow it at all or just mow a path through it. Not only are these features low maintenance, they are also more beneficial to wildlife. For other low-maintenance options for lawns, see pp.128–29.

Should I create a garden diary?

Clients often ask me to create a planting maintenance schedule to help them to look after their gardens or to give to the gardener if they have one. To create one, simply list each type of plant in the garden and write the maintenance it needs from January through to December. Of course, for many months, some plants may not need any maintenance at all. Alternatively, you could divide your diary into monthly sections and write down the tasks that you must carry out in the garden each month.

You can also include notes about how to prune your plants under the relevant month. For example, wisteria is pruned in late summer and again in late winter. In late summer you prune stems back to six buds from a main stem; in late winter you prune back further to three buds. You can also make notes of any plants that are susceptible to pests or diseases and how these can be dealt with.

Include information about when to mulch your borders, clean the water feature or pond, apply a spring and autumn lawn feed and weed product, propagate certain plants, sow seeds of annuals or vegetables, and plant bulbs. You may also like to include a reminder of when to order your seeds or bulbs.

It is useful to note down the successes and failures that you have had, too.

Collating all this information will help to build your knowledge of how to look after your garden until it becomes second nature.

How do I maintain my planting borders?

Including a vast variety of different plants in the garden is good for biodiversity but it can create more work throughout the seasons. So, if you want to limit the time spent maintaining your borders, you can make the following choices:

- Plant more slow-growing shrubs.
- If you opt for hedging, select slow-growing varieties that need cutting just once a year.
- Limiting your palette of plants and repeating the planting will also reduce the maintenance tasks throughout the year.
- Choose plants that do not require a lot of maintenance such as ornamental grasses, which only need cutting back once in spring before the new growth is emerging.

- Mulch your planting borders (see p.186). This reduces evaporation and helps to suppress weeds.
- Clip, prune and shape your shrubs, hedges and structural plants at the correct times of the year. Avoid letting them get out of shape.
- Carry out any pruning and spraying on trees at the correct times of the year for the particular species.
- Weed little and often, collecting a handful every time you go out. However, remember weeds are often just plants and flowers in the wrong place, so bear in mind that dandelions are a rich source of food for many of our pollinators before removing them all.

A tip for slugs and snails
Some gardeners have had success by watering their tender plants with a solution of garlic water. Boil 5-6 garlic cloves in about 1.8 litres/60fl oz water, then allow to cool. Mix 4-5 tablespoons of this solution per 5 litres of water in a can and water your tender plants with this. The water can also be used in a sprayer bottle to spray the leaves. Worth a try as it is chemical free.

About the author

Manoj Malde [Mald-é] is an award-winning garden designer and TV gardener, known for his vibrant style and bold use of colour. Manoj is best known for his presenting work on the BBC garden show *Your Garden Made Perfect* and Channel 4's *Garden Of The Year*, where his infectious enthusiasm has made him a hugely popular part of the programmes. Manoj is also an RHS show judge, RHS ambassador and Chelsea Flower Show medallist.

Manoj attributes his love of colour to his Indian ancestry, as well as his background within the fashion industry, where he worked for 18 years. As a former creative director, with a master's degree in fashion design from the Royal College of Art, Manoj is highly skilled at combining textures and colours within planting schemes. Manoj describes the design processes behind bespoke gardens and fashion as similar, starting out with themes, mood boards, colour palettes and textures. 'Designing a planting scheme is like creating a beautiful silk print,' he says. 'I've gone from haute couture to 'hort' couture.'

Thank yous

Clive Gillmor – my husband for keeping me grounded, having patience with me to pursue my goals, and always believing in me.

My family – for always supporting me in my work, career and taking pride in my achievements.

Mary Malde – for be being my creative mirror.

Tecwyn Evans and Gareth Wilson – two of my besties & ace landscape contractors. Your guidance has always been appreciated.

Simon Pyle – the gentleman who set me on my garden design journey. 'You will go straight to Chelsea my boy.'

Rosemary Alexander – for her never-ending support.

Borra Garson and Jan Croxson at DML Talent – for making me realise my worth.

Picture credits

Garden design: **David Loy, Your Garden Design** 175t, 195br, 199.

Detail of garden designed by **Declan Buckley at Buckley Design Associates**, photo **MMGI/Marianne Majerus** 65bl, 84, 145br, 161t, 189bl; photo **Rachel Warne** 146br, 162b.

Garden design: **Eliza Gray Gardens** 136, 154t, 170; and photo: **Chris Sami** 178tl.

Garden design: **greencube design** 16b, 18t; 95b; 99tr; 186; 189tr; 191t.

Garden design: **James Lee, James Lee Design** 18bl, 61b, 75l, 78; and photo: **Anthony Coleman** 61b; **Trevor Lahiff Architects/photo by MMGI/Marianne Majerus** 63.

Garden design: **Jane Bingham at The Cheshire Garden** 128–129c.

Garden design: **Jane Brockbank Gardens**, photo: **MMGI/Marianne Majerus** 141t.

Garden design: **Stephen Firth and Brinsbury students** – Chelsea 2005, photo: **Jonathan Buckley**: 87b.

Garden design: **Jennifer Gay**, photo: **MMGI/Marianne Majerus** 165b.

Garden design: **Jilayne Rickards Contemporary Garden Design**, photo: **Simon Bourne** 58, 104

Garden design: **Joanna Archer Garden Design**: 80b.

Garden design: **Lucy Willcox Garden Design**: 12, 16t, 70t; and photo **@agatamillerphotography** 31t.

Garden design: **Maïtanne Hunt**, photo: **Joanna Kossak** 176.

Garden design: **Mark Fenton Designs**, **Brooks-Carter Photography**: 110l, 174b.

Garden design: **Martha Krempel Garden Design**: Trees for Privacy, for a

front garden in North London 83r; and 'Secret Garden', London NW2, photo: **Julian Caldwell** 20t.

Garden design: **Murphy + Sheanon Horticulture & Landscape Architecture, Ireland**, photo: **MMGI/Marianne Majerus** 96

Garden design: **Natasha Nuttall Garden Design** 88, 146tr; and photo: **Ellie Walpole**: 20b; **MMGI/Bennet Smith** 61t, 192.

Garden design: **Neil Sutcliffe**: 81tl.

Garden design: **Nigel Philips, One-to-One Garden Design** 67b.

Garden design: **Noel Kingsbury**, photo: **MMGI/Marianne Majerus** 165t.

Sussex Prairie Garden, Sussex, garden design: **Paul and Pauline McBride**, photo: **MMGI/Marianne Majerus** 157t.

Garden design: **Peter Donegan Garden Design**, photo: **Luke Cleary Photography for RTE Television**: 60b.

Garden design: **Rachel Bailey** 95t, 166b.

Garden design: **Robert Hughes Garden Design**: Landscaper = WM Exteriors 14; Landscaper = Greenbelt 115b; Landscaper = Brockstone Landscape Construction 146tl; Landscaper = Walmsley Shaw 189br; and Landscaper = Brockstone Landscape Construction, photographer = **Kevin Elias** 99tl;

Garden design: **Sara Jane Rothwell**, photo: **MMGI/Marianne Majerus** 81tr.

Garden design: **Sarah Kay Garden Design** 65tl; and photo: **Ellie Walpole** 85, 91tr.

Garden design: **Stephen Gore** 9; 108; 110–111c; 151t; 151b; 153tr; 153br; 168.

Garden design: **Steve Edney**, photo: **MMGI/Marianne Majerus** 162b.

Garden design: **Tara Dalton Garden Design**, photo: **MMGI/Bennet Smith** 147.

Garden design: **Sue Whittington**, photo: **MMGI/Marianne Majerus** 158t.
Garden design: **Susan Willmott and Adele Ford**, photo: **MMGI/Marianne Majerus** 166t.

Garden design: **Tom Howard**, photo: **Joanna Kossak** 60t.

Garden design: **Tim Austen garden designer**: www.timaustengardendesigns.com 80t, 81bl, 195t.

Garden design: **Ula Maria**: 68t.

Photography: **Manoj Malde**: 76, 173, 177.

Photography: **MMGI/Marianne Majerus** 141b, 144tc, 158b, 161b; The Old Vicarage, East Ruston, Norfolk 137t; Beth Chatto Gardens, Essex 137b; Grafton Cottage, Staffordshire 157b.

And thanks also to these sources: **Alamy**, and the following: John Keates 22; Garden design: Manoj Malde/Photo: Ellen Rooney 23b; Imagebroker 28b; Garden design: Manoj Malde/Photo: Guy Bell 33l; UK City Images 144bc; Garden design: Manoj Malde/Photo: Andrew Lalchan 175b.

GAP Photos: 18br, 115tl, 126tr, 131b, 133, 171b, 184t; and the following: Howard Rice – Design: Adam frost 4; Annaick Guitteny 17, 107c; Dave Zubraski 21t, 29 row 4 left; Leigh Clapp – Designer: Victoria Truman 21bl; Clare Forbes – Designer: Matt Keightley. Sponsor: The David Brownlow Charitable Foundation 21br; Nicola Stocken – Designer: David Ward 25tr; Tim Gainey 29 row 1; Ernie Janes 29 row 2 left; Sarah Cuttle 29 row 2 right, 121; Jonathan Buckley 29 row 3; Pernilla Bergdahl 29 row 4 r; Heather Edwards – Design: Ula Maria 62; Stephen Studd – Designer: Kate Gould 65br; J S Sira 67c; Brent Wilson 70b, 100, 125br, 195bl; Elke Borkowski 72b, 153tl; Nicola Stocken 73, 91b, 113, 143l, 143c, 174t; Perry Mastrovito 75r, 140; Paul Debois – Design by The Distinctive Gardener 77r; Perry Mastrovito – Centre

Index

Directory

I encourage you to seek out local, trustworthy suppliers, as well as using marketplaces and upcycling where possible. Here are some suggestions for suppliers to get you started.

ARCHITECTURAL SALVAGE YARDS

Ashwells Reclaimed Tropical Timber
ashwelltimber.com

English Salvage Ltd
englishsalvage.co.uk

Nostalgia & New
nostalgiaandnew.com

V&V Reclamation
vandv.co.uk

BULBS

Farmer Gracey
farmergracy.co.uk

J Parker's
jparkers.co.uk

Jacques Amand International
jacquesamandintl.com

DECKING

Jewson
jewson.co.uk

Millboard Decking
millboard.co.uk

Woodtrend
woodtrend.co.uk

FENCING

Jackson's Fencing
jacksons-fencing.co.uk

Travis Perkins
travisperkins.co.uk

FURNITURE

Alexander Rose
alexander-rose.co.uk

Barlow Tyrie
barlow.worldofteak.co.uk

Garden 4 Less
garden4less.co.uk

Garden Furniture
gardenfurniture.co.uk

Whitestores
whitestores.co.uk

GARDEN SHEDS

The Cosy Shed Co
thecosyshedco.co.uk

DenSheds Ltd
densheds.co.uk

Dunster House
dunsterhouse.co.uk

The Posh Shed Company
theposhshedcompany.co.uk

Shed Store
shedstore.co.uk

LIGHTS

Landscapeplus
landscapeplus.com

Lighting for Gardens
lightingforgardens.com

Lighting Direct
lighting-direct.co.uk

NURSERIES

Beth Chatto
bethchatto.co.uk

Claire Austin Hardy Plants
claireaustin-hardyplants.co.uk

Hayloft
hayloft.co.uk

Kelways
kelways.co.uk

OUTDOOR KITCHENS

Grillo Living
grilloliving.com

My Outdoor Kitchen
myoutdoorkitchen.co.uk

Wwoo Outdoor Kitchen
wwoo.nl

PAINTS

Earthborn Paints
earthbornpaints.co.uk

Thorndown Paints
thorndown.co.uk

Valspar, sold at B&Q
diy.com

PERGOLAS

Pergola
pergola.co.uk

Tuin
tuin.co.uk

Whitestores
whitestores.co.uk

PIZZA OVENS

Gozney
gozney.com/pages/home-pizza-ovens

Ooni Pizza Ovens
uk.ooni.com

POTS

Get Potted
getpotted.com

Pots & Pithoi
potsandpithoi.com

Wool Pots
wool-pots.co.uk

World of Pots
worldofpots.com

SCREENS

Brampton Willows
bramptonwillows.co.uk

Charles and Ivy
charlesandivy.co.uk

Screens with Envy
screenwithenvy.co.uk

Stark and Greensmith
starkandgreensmith.com

SEED SUPPLIERS

Chiltern Seeds
chilternseeds.co.uk

Higgledy Garden
higgledygarden.com

Mr Fothergill's
mr-fothergills.co.uk

Suttons
suttons.co.uk

STONE PAVERS PORCELAIN

CED Stone
cedstone.co.uk

London Stone
londonstone.co.uk

Schellevis
schellevis.nl/nl/home

Vande Moortel
vandemoortel.be

Further reading

GENERAL GARDENING

- *The Complete & Practical Guide to Patio, Terrace, Backyard & Courtyard Gardening* by Joan Clifton and Jenny Hendy
- *The Creative Shrub Garden* by Andy McIndoe
- *The Dry Gardening Handbook* by Olivier Filippe
- *Gardening Through the Year* by Ian Spence
- *Late Summer Flowers* by Marina Christopher
- *Perfect Plant, Perfect Place* by Roy Lancaster
- *Planting Design for Dry Gardens* by Olivier Filippe
- *RHS Encyclopaedia of Gardening* edited by Christopher Brickell
- *RHS Pests & Diseases* by Pippa Greenwood & Andrew Halstead
- *RHS Pruning & Training* by Christopher Brickell and David Joyce
- *What to sow, grow and do* by Benjamin Pope

GROWING FRUIT & VEGETABLES

- *Grow Your Own Veg* by Carol Klein
- *Vegetable & Fruit Gardening* edited by Michael Pollock

TREES

- *Collins Tree Guide* by Owen Johnson & David More

SUSTAINABLE GARDENING

- *High Impact, Low Carbon Gardening* by Alice Bowe
- *Resilient Garden* by Tom Massey
- *Sustainable Garden* by Marian Boswell

GARDEN DESIGN

- *The Art of the Islamic Garden* by Emma Clarke
- *The Essential Garden Design Workbook* by Rosemary Alexander
- *The Garden in Winter* by Rosemary Verey
- *New Small Garden* by Noel Kingsbury
- *Small Gardens* by John Brookes

COLOUR

- *Chromatopia* by David Coles
- *Colour by Design* by Nori and Sandra Pope
- *Colour Psychology Today* by June McLeod
- *The Gardener's Book of Colour* by Andrew Wilson
- *Little Book of Colour* by Karen Haller
- *The Secret Lives of Colour* by Kassia St Clair

BOOKS TO INSPIRE

This list is by no means exhaustive. Here are a few of my personal favourites that I turn to for inspiration on certain themes:

- *The Art of the Islamic Garden* by Emma Clark
- *Avant Gardeners* by Tim Richardson
- *Barragán* by Armand Salas Portugal
- *Desert Eves: An Indian Paradise* by Catherine Clément
- *Desert Gardens* of Steve Martino by Caren Yglesias
- *Garden & Cosmos – The Royal Paintings of Jodhpur* by The British Museum
- *Hip Hotels* by Thames and Hudson
- *India Style* by Suzanne Slesin & Stafford Cliff
- *The Last of the Maasai* by Mohamed Amin, Duncan Willets and John Eames
- *Living Bright: Fashioning Colourful Interiors* by Matthew Williamson and Michelle Ogundehin
- *Maasai* by Tepilit Ole Saitoti
- *Mediterranean Landscape Design* by Louisa Jones
- *The Mid-Century Modern Garden* by Ethne Clark
- *Nndebele* by Margaret Courtney-Clarke
- *Paradise Gardens* by Arnaud Maurières & Éric Ossart
- *Textile Arts of India* by Kokyo Hatanaka
- *Vanishing Africa* by Mirella Ricciardi
- *Villas & Courtyard Houses of Moroccco* by Corinne Verner

Of course, books are not the only source of inspiration; getting out and about to visit galleries, museums, exhibitions and gardens will always prove hugely inspirational.

Quarto

First published in 2024 by Frances Lincoln,
an imprint of The Quarto Group.
One Triptych Place, London, SE1 9SH,
United Kingdom
T (0)20 7700 9000
www.Quarto.com

A catalogue record for this book is available from the British Library.

ISBN 978-0-7112-8224-7
Ebook ISBN 978-0-7112-8225-4

10 9 8 7 6 5 4 3 2 1

Publisher: Philip Cooper
Commissioning Editor: Alice Graham
Project Editor: Melissa Smith
Senior Editor: Laura Bulbeck
Art Director: Paileen Currie
Designer: Sarah Pyke
Picture Research: Laura Bulbeck and Katerina Menhennet
Production Controller: Rohana Yusof

Printed in China